FENCES, T
AND SCREENS

GARDEN MATTERS

FENCES, TRELLISES AND SCREENS

PETER McHOY

WARD LOCK

First published in Great Britain in 1992
by Ward Lock Limited, Villiers House,
41/47 Strand, London WC2N 5JE, England

A Cassell Imprint

© Ward Lock Limited

Text filmset in 11/11½ point ITC Garamond Light
by Columns of Reading
Printed and bound in Great Britain
by HarperCollins Book Manufacturing, Glasgow

British Library Cataloguing in Publication Data

McHoy, Peter, *1941–*
Fences, trellises and screens. – (Garden
matters)
I. Title II. Series
717

ISBN 07063 7039 2

CONTENTS

INTRODUCTION

The garden boundary may at first thought seem a rather uninteresting – even boring – aspect of gardening, yet it actually has a profound impact on a garden's structure and sense of design. Hedges, fences and walls define shapes and areas, and act as a backdrop for plants in beds and borders, as well as having very practical purposes such as hiding what needs to be hidden (oil storage tanks, compost and work areas, or simply an unpleasant view). You may have bought this book for a purely practical reason, perhaps for advice on repairing a fence, or to find a quick screen to hide some ugly sight beyond or within a new garden, but before you put the book down I hope that you will see that the garden boundary is actually an opportunity for really creative gardening. Fences, hedges, and screens can have as much impact on the garden as beds and borders, and they can give a quite modest and ordinary garden a strong sense of 'design'.

Gardeners often give much time and thought to flower beds, yet it is often the boundaries and internal dividers that have the most effect on the overall impression of the garden – and the smaller the garden the more true this is. Many modern gardens are so small that the fence or hedge always intrudes on the scene, and a neglected fence or an overgrown hedge will mar the most brilliant border. Conversely, a really splendid wall, a fence of character, or an interesting hedge, can make a distinctive and interesting contribution, even if the planting within the garden is modest.

In a large garden, internal screens and hedges are useful for they can give it shape, a sense of line, or be a feature in their own right (a 'walk' flanked by a formal hedge, maybe with topiary, for instance). Even a garden of modest size can often be made more interesting by dividing it up into small 'rooms' so that you can't take in the whole garden at a glance and have to wander around to explore it.

Whether replacing an old hedge or fence, or considering a new one, it makes sense to think creatively as well as in practical terms.

PRACTICAL POINTERS

Internal hedges and dividers are generally primarily design features, but boundary hedges and fences often have to be functional too. Keeping animals and children in – or out – is the most common consideration, providing privacy another. But they are also useful in less obvious ways – they can filter traffic noise, prevent litter blowing into the garden, and even cut down the amount of pollutants such as lead from entering your garden and contaminating vegetables, if you live near a very busy road.

Hedges, in particular, are useful as windbreaks, reducing the damage to other plants and generally providing shelter that makes the garden that much milder and more pleasant.

The choice of boundary can have a profound effect on how labour-intensive or low-maintenance the garden is to run. Along with the lawn, hedges can be very labour-intensive; walls and fences are low-maintenance but relatively expensive initially.

The chapters in this book will guide you through the pros and cons of the various types of boundaries and screens, to help you make the right choice for *your* garden. And the practical step-by-step instructions will tell you how to achieve the best results.

CHAPTER 1

FENCES

Almost any modern housing development will reveal a forest of timber fences, all very similar and all rather boring; the same gardens a few years later will have been softened by the growth of plants, but now the fences, instead of looking clean and bright, will probably have weathered to an uninspiring silvery-grey unless they have been conscientiously treated with a preservative. Anyone who has bought a new property will be glad of the instant privacy that a wooden fence can provide, but plain fencing panels and closeboard fencing do not do justice to the many other fine fences of character that can be created with timber and other materials. Do not dismiss a fence simply because some look boring or unimaginative.

If you require a functional and practical fence that is inexpensive to buy and easy to erect, fencing panels are ideal (and they can be enhanced with suitable plants), but where a sense of character and design is important, some of the alternatives suggested in this chapter are worth considering.

Fences have many advantages: the effect is immediate, they are much cheaper than walls and easier to erect; they require considerably less maintenance than hedges (though more than for walls); and there are styles and materials to suit most pockets and situations. The drawback is that many can look common-place and they require at least some maintenance to keep them in good condition.

The main advantages of a fence are instant cover and privacy for less cost than a brick or concrete wall, and quick and easy erection.

The main disadvantages come with age. Wooden fences can begin to look jaded, and as the timber shrinks gaps may begin to appear in panel and close-board types. Fences that do not deteriorate with time, such as concrete, generally lack visual appeal.

CHOOSING A FENCE

The best fence for a given situation is one that is visually acceptable yet practical for its purpose. The latter is most important, for if you want privacy it must be peep-proof (and high enough!); if you want to keep animals in or out, it must do that efficiently. No matter how attractive a fence may look, if it does not do the job required it will be a constant source of irritation. To help decide which is realistically likely to suit your needs, the descriptions that follow point out potential problems as well as advantages.

TIMBER FENCES

Chestnut paling/Split chestnut paling

This is made from roughly split vertical pales spaced about 7.5 cm (3 in) apart, held together by two or three bands of galvanized wire. It is widely used by contractors for temporary fencing.

Good for a cheap short-term fence, perhaps while a hedge grows, or to provide a degree of protection from animals while shrubs are becoming established (it lets light in and does not cast the rain-shadow created by more solid fences). Also invaluable as a temporary boundary marker or enclosure for many animals, though it should be remembered that it will not keep out small animals such as rabbits.

Bad for appearance. Nobody could describe chestnut paling as attractive. In time the wire will rust and the fence disintegrate, but as it is not intended as a permanent fence, chestnut paling will almost certainly last long enough for its intended use.

Buying and erecting. This type of fence must be purchased ready-made and is widely available from local fencing companies.

Closeboard

This type of fence is popular with builders, and it has similar properties to a panel fence. Although quick and easy for a builder or contractor to erect, closeboard fences are more trouble than panel fences to erect yourself, as they are assembled on site and require expert carpentry skills. The vertical slats, nailed to horizontal rails, overlap one another slightly, and are usually feather-edged for a neater finish. A horizontal gravel board (Fig. 1) is usually fitted at ground level so that if soil and moisture are in contact with the fence, it is the gravel board that will rot and not the main fence.

Good for privacy and security. Although privacy is determined by height, closeboard fences are peep-proof and will provide an adequate barrier for all but the most agile or determined of animals (such as cats).

Bad for creating a strong sense of character or design. Although very practical, closeboard fencing can look boring, especially if there is a lot of it in the immediate vicinity.

Buying and erecting. Any fencing contractor will quickly erect this type of fence for you, or you can buy the posts, rails and boards from a fencing supplier. Some d-i-y stores also stock suitable posts and feather-edged boards. Fig. 13 (page 40) shows how the fence is assembled. See page 33 for details of inserting posts (generally you must use wooden posts unless you can find concrete posts with the required mortises).

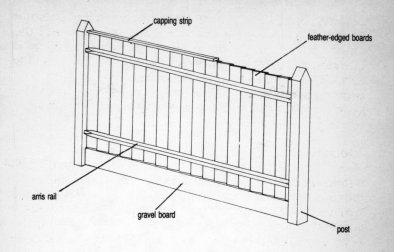

Fig. 1 *Closeboard fences are widely used on new housing estates, because they offer a high degree of security and an element of privacy.*

Interference/interlap

Although oddly named, this is actually an attractive fence that will give your garden a strong sense of design (Fig. 2). 'Interference' is usually used to describe fencing with horizontal square-edged boards that over-lap on opposite sides of vertical supports; 'interlap' is usually used to describe similar fencing with vertical slats. You may find both kinds of fence described by other names, such as 'hit-and-miss', which better describes their visual appearance. The planks are nailed to both sides of the supports, and the degree of overlap determines the amount of privacy provided – the greater the overlap and therefore the more timber used, the more peep-proof the fence.

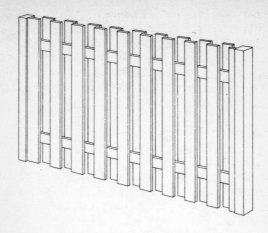

Fig. 2 *Interlap fences are not totally peep-proof, but provide a much better environment for plants. The wind is filtered rather than being obstructed so there is less damaging turbulence. Horizontal planks may be tempting for children to climb; vertical planks are more satisfactory in this respect.*

Good for creating a strong sense of design, with more character than most timber fences. But to make a feature of this type of fence it needs to be treated with a good timber preservative and stain every year. It is a much better windbreak than a solid fence, as it filters the wind rather than creating turbulence.

Bad for cost. A good fence of this kind needs very strong supports, quite substantial timbers for the boards, and because they are unlikely to be available mass-produced, the cost is likely to be more than an equivalent panel fence, for instance. Also, fences of this type are usually made tall for privacy (though you may still see through them if viewed at an angle), which increases the amount of timber required. Some people find this type of fence too 'solid' and a trifle oppressive, especially in a small garden. Children may be tempted to climb fencing with spaced horizontal boards.

Buying and erecting. This is really a d-i-y job, and a good timber merchant is likely to be able to supply the necessary timber.

Palisade see **Picket,** p. 18.

Panel fences

These are justifiably popular – they are quick and easy to erect, relatively simple to repair or replace if necessary, and are very practical in terms of privacy and security (Fig. 3).

The prefabricated panels simply slot between concrete posts or are screwed to timber posts (see step-by-step instructions on page 37).

The panels may have horizontal or vertical overlapping slats, sometimes with a waney edge to produce a more rustic look; interwoven panels have thin strips of wood interwoven like a basket weave (these are less peep-proof as there are often gaps between the strips). Trellis panels are also available, to use instead of solid panels or between them where you want to grow climbers.

Smaller trellis strips, sometimes attractively curved, are available to fix on top of solid panel fences, and these often add a lot of character, especially if you also introduce a couple of suitable climbers.

Good for speed and simplicity of erection, easy availability, security and (generally) peep-proof qualities. *Bad* for strength. These are often the first fences to be damaged in a severe gale, though much depends on the quality of manufacture and how well they have been erected. Can be a little boring if too many panel fences are used in your area.

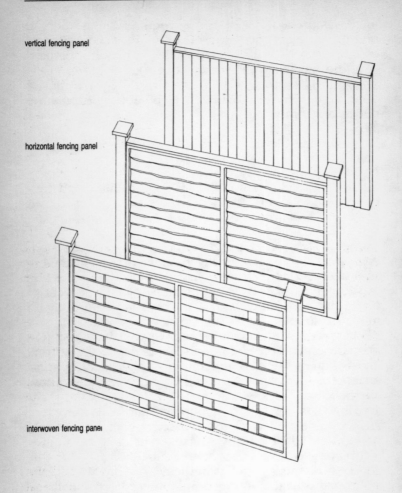

vertical fencing panel

horizontal fencing panel

interwoven fencing panel

Fig. 3 *Panel fencing is widely available and is very quick and easy to erect. The panels vary in design, horizontal timbers being the most common, but there are vertical and interwoven patterns too.*

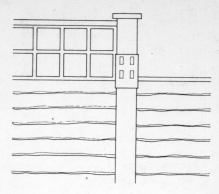

Fig. 4 *A trellis extension is a good way to increase the height of a panel fence, and can look very attractive when covered with a climber. Metal extension brackets are available that make them easy to fix to an existing fence.*

<u>*Buying and erecting.*</u> Although erection is an easy d-i-y job, the panels must be bought. They are available from most garden centres, timber merchants, fencing contractors, d-i-y superstores, and by mail order. The quality varies considerably from make to make, so try to see the fencing panels to assess quality before you order.

Step-by-step instructions for erecting a panel fence are given on page 37.

It is easier to incorporate trellis extensions when the fence is erected (Fig. 4), because you simply add the appropriate height to the posts, but you can buy metal brackets to extend an existing fence – you just remove the post cap, slip on the joining piece, pop the appropriate extension post into the top, and refix the cap to this.

Picket/palisade

These are charming in the right setting, and can produce a delightful cottage-garden feel to the garden if painted white and maintained in good condition (Fig. 5). They have closely spaced vertical slats nailed to two or three horizontal bars. The top of each slat is generally pointed, sometimes spear-shaped, but can be rounded or shaped more ornately.

Good for a decorative fence that will keep out larger animals and children. This type of fence can be a feature in its own right.

Bad for privacy. These fences are generally relatively low – about 1–1.2 m (3–4 ft) high – and in any case are not peep-proof. As they look best when painted, they require more maintenance than most other fences (it's

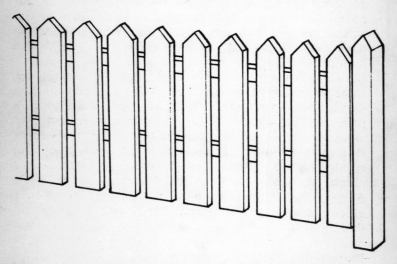

Fig. 5 *Picket fencing is one of the most attractive types where a low decorative boundary marker is required. Stain it a natural wood colour or paint it white for a really smart effect.*

worth washing down the paintwork each year, even if you don't repaint annually). A plastic version (see page 23) will cut down on the maintenance.

Buying and erecting. You can buy these fences as self-assembly kits or ready-assembled panels, but as relatively small sections of timber are used, it's an easy project for any competent d-i-y enthusiast.

Post-and-rail

This can make a simple, relatively inexpensive and unobtrusive fence in the right setting. It is the kind of fence often used to keep horses or livestock in, but makes an acceptable fence for a large garden in a rural setting. For a town garden, a ranch-style fence (see page 23) is more appropriate. Post-and-rail fences have one or more horizontal bars or rails (often round or half round and usually oak or larch) fixed between round or square posts (usually oak or chestnut). The rails may be nailed to the posts or notched into them, though the method of fixing can vary.

Good for boundary markers, especially in a rural setting, where privacy is not important. Relatively inexpensive.

Bad for security. They are fine for keeping horses in a paddock, but are useless as a barrier for smaller animals, such as dogs, rabbits and other creatures that you may want to keep out. It won't keep balls and children out of the garden – children may use it as a climbing frame.

Buying and erecting. Post-and-rail fences are usually erected on site, and any good fencing contractor can do this for you.

Ranch-style fences.   See page 23.

METAL FENCES

Metal sounds an unlikely material for fences, but of

course there are various forms of wire mesh that can be used, or traditional railings. Although some mesh fences have a relatively short life, they generally require little or no maintenance, and you certainly won't have the cost and effort of applying a preservative periodically. Railings can last a lifetime.

Mesh fences

These never look inspired, but they are practical boundary markers and, depending on the size of the mesh, will keep out most animals.

Generally made from galvanized or plastic-coated steel, the wires are interlocked or welded together (welded meshes are usually the more robust). **Chain-link** fencing is one of the best for general garden use, and is very robust if properly erected (Fig. 6).

Good for security (if high enough); excellent for keeping dogs in (or out).

Bad for appearance, though it can often be screened effectively with shrubs. There is no privacy.

Buying and erecting. Fencing suppliers are the most likely source of supply (if you have difficulty, the manufacturer will be able to advise). Erection is not a difficult d-i-y job if you follow the manufacturer's instructions. The mesh must be tensioned on wires stretched between secure posts. Screwed eye-bolts can be used to tension the line wires between concrete or timber posts, but stretcher bars, strainer bars and winding brackets may be required. Some manufacturers use angle-iron for the supports. Special posts may be required for corners and end pieces, so make sure you know exactly how much fence you require, and how many corner pieces are needed, before you talk to the supplier.

Fine-mesh wire of other kinds can be used where very small animals have to be contained, but this may have to be fixed within a timber frame for rigidity and security.

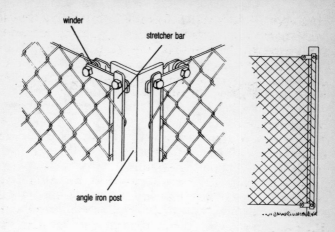

Fig. 6 *Chain link fences are not especially attractive (though they can be clothed with climbers such as ivy or screened with shrubs), but they are excellent for providing a secure barrier against animals and children.*

Post and chain

These 'fences' are symbolic boundary markers, and as the posts are made of wood or plastic, and the 'chains' are likely to be plastic rather than metal nowadays, this type of fence is difficult to classify. The square posts, usually wooden, are spaced at intervals with the chain draped between them. They can look good as a boundary marker in an open-plan garden where a more substantial boundary marker may not be allowed.

Good for marking a boundary where a hedge or fence would be inappropriate or not allowed. Not expensive and easy to make yourself.

Bad for protection or privacy of any kind – they are purely symbolic markers.

<u>*Buying and erecting.*</u> Easy to make yourself. You can

use ordinary fencing posts cut to size, and the hooks and chains can be bought from good hardware stores and some garden centres.

Railings

It is easy to assume that metal railings are only for old Victorian houses or public parks. Certainly they need using with care, and may look ostentatious among a row of houses with simple privet hedges or closeboard fencing; but in the right setting they will add a touch of elegance and taste that you will never achieve with a timber fence, nor even with most hedges.

You can indulge yourself with railings of many designs, including spearheads, fleurs-de-lys, and some with cast finials; or you can keep it plain and simple. Traditionally the metal used would have been a ferrous metal, but nowadays it is likely to be an aluminium alloy, which is light and low-maintenance.

Good for security and a touch of elegance.

Bad for privacy; requires the right setting; and relatively expensive.

Buying and erecting. You are unlikely to find metal railings in local stores and garden centres, as many are hand-made by craftsmen working on a small scale. Some advertise nationally in gardening and lifestyle magazines; others may advertise regionally, so try the classified telephone directory. Follow the manufacturer's advice for erecting.

Wire-netting

This is not a practical proposition for a fence, even a low one, as it is simply too short-term, besides being visually unacceptable on its own; but it is useful for short-term protection. It is a cheap and practical barrier against many animals while a hedge is becoming established; and may be desirable at the base of an established hedge if you want to keep small animals in or out.

Good for keeping small animals in or out, and may even provide some protection against litter blowing into your garden while a hedge is becoming established.

Bad for visual appearance, and will rust through after a few years.

Buying and erecting. Wire-netting can be bought from most hardware stores, as well as some garden centres and from builders' merchants. It is inexpensive, and a large mesh is usually adequate and helps to reduce the cost. It is sold in rolls in a selection of heights. Simply nail or staple it to battens or posts driven into the ground – the size of these will depend on the height of the netting and strength required.

PLASTIC FENCES

Plastic should not be dismissed as a fencing material. Some plastics are a practical low-maintenance substitute for timber.

Ranch-style

These fences are traditionally made of wood and painted white (though they can be left a natural colour); nowadays plastic versions are widely available and are generally a more practical option than a painted fence (Fig. 7). A good make, with plastic treated to resist deterioration in sunlight, will last for many years; these are not a cheap option, but bear in mind that you will not have the cost of regular painting. You can simply wash down the white plastic periodically, and they look very convincing.

Ranch-style fences are more compact versions of the post-and-rail fence. Horizontal wooden or plastic planks, usually about 8–15 cm (3–6 in) wide and well spaced apart, are fixed to posts spaced at about 1.8 m (6 ft) intervals. Height varies, but about 1 m (3 ft) looks right for most small front gardens.

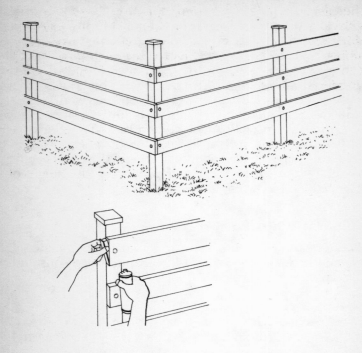

Fig. 7 *Ranch-style fencing is smart for town or country. Although white-painted wood is traditional for this type of fence, modern plastic versions are very convincing and can be kept clean and smart with little maintenance.*

Good for a smart finish at moderate cost and, in the case of the plastic version, low maintenance too.
Bad for privacy and security. These are purely ornamental fences.
<u>*Buying and erecting.*</u> Timber ranch-style fences are usually d-i-y jobs, and you make the fence on site. Plastic versions are bought as kits, which are easily assembled.

The pieces can be cut to length with a hacksaw fitted with a coarse blade, and can be drilled easily where necessary. All the pieces and bolts required are usually supplied. Plastic posts and 'boards' are capped or sealed with post caps and end caps fixed with a solvent-weld adhesive.

CHAPTER 2

SOMETHING DIFFERENT

The most widely available types of fence are generally the best – that's why they are popular. They are widely used either because they look good or because they do a practical job cheaply in comparison with some of the more sophisticated alternatives; so do not choose something different just for the sake of being different.

Sometimes, however, the less traditional fences can be just right for a particular setting. Maybe an internal screen within the garden calls for a more aesthetically pleasing material; conversely in an area that is not normally seen you may want something strong and secure – such as concrete – even though you would not choose it for a more prominent position. Although not an exhaustive list, some of the following ideas for 'alternative' fences may appeal for a particular situation.

CONCRETE FENCES

These usually sound particularly unattractive to anyone who has never seen them, but they do have their uses. They are very robust, absolutely peep-proof, and generally require no maintenance (though you may want to paint them with an exterior wall paint). They are usually assembled as relatively small (though still very heavy) panels that slot between concrete posts, and the fence is built up to the required height in this way. Some simply have an exposed aggregate finish, but you

Fig. 8 *Concrete fences are excellent where security is important, and from the side with a decorative finish can be surprisingly acceptable visually.*

can obtain some that resemble brickwork – at much less cost than the real thing.

A concrete fence (Fig. 8) is worth considering if you want good security, perhaps blocking an unattractive outlook at the same time; and it can be softened with plants – self-clinging climbers such as ivies are ideal. Wall shrubs planted in front are also very effective, and if you paint the fence a pale colour, this will often help to show off the plants.

It is essential that the concrete posts are very firmly set before sliding in the heavy panels, so allow at least a week.

Finally, it is worth considering your neighbours before choosing a concrete fence, as the opposite side to the one with the attractive finish may be plain and not particularly pleasing to look at!

PLASTIC PANELS

This is the type of suggestion that usually raises a few eyebrows, but in a few special circumstances see-through plastic panels can be a practical proposition. Think about them where you want to enjoy a terrific view, but need a screen for safety or protection (perhaps because the land drops away, or simply for wind protection). You can then still enjoy the view in a way that would be impossible with hedges and most fences (most of those that you can see through easily offer little protection or shelter). They are also worth considering around a swimming pool area – for safety you may need to fence off the swimming pool, yet a see-through screen enables you to continue to enjoy the view while achieving shelter for yourself, and a degree of security and protection so that children and animals are less likely to fall in the pool.

Perspex and other glass substitutes are available from good d-i-y stores as well as specialist plastics suppliers, but you will have to make a timber framework into which the panels can be slotted. They must be secured firmly, as this kind of panel offers a lot of wind resistance.

REED AND BAMBOO SCREENS

These are useful for providing a backdrop *within* the garden, but they are not widely available and are not very durable. However they are ideal as a background for, say, a corner of the garden with a Japanese-style influence, and can be useful for screening oil storage tanks, dustbins and their like.

Reed screens can sometimes be bought from garden centres, but you could make your own bamboo fence for an informal part of the garden. By securing stout canes (much thicker than those normally used as plant supports) with wire or thick string, a charming informal 'fence' can be constructed. The bamboos are spaced quite far apart for this type of fence, and should not be confused with a reed or bamboo screen where the reeds or canes form a continuous ribbon.

RAILWAY SLEEPERS

Suggested here as an example of how a little thought can produce a fence of distinction from unlikely material. A low fence can be made by sinking the sleepers into the ground end-on – you can keep them all at the same height, or vary the height of each one to add a touch of character to an already distinctive fence.

Always try to match the style of fence to the style of garden: this 'chunky' effect, for instance, would look wrong in a pretty cottage garden, or one intensively planted with the emphasis on flowers, but it can look great in a garden of simple style where line and form hold the garden together rather than the plants.

For a low fence, each sleeper can be cut in half (which makes the job cheaper) and this will also require less excavation as at least a third of each one must be set in the ground for stability. It may be necessary to ram hardcore around the base, and if the soil is unstable pack it with a concrete mix.

SHINGLE

This makes an uncommon fence in the UK, though they are more often seen in countries such as the USA (Fig. 9). The shingles are small wooden tiles, like those seen on some summerhouses, and are made of a durable wood such as cedar. They are nailed in staggered rows to a framework of stout timber (or you can 'convert' an old fence by nailing them to this). The bottom row is fixed first so that each subsequent row overlaps the

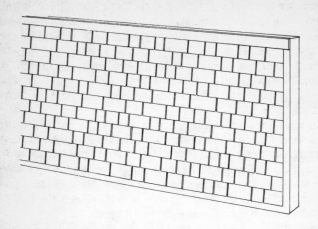

Fig. 9 *Shingle fences are very uncommon in the UK, but in some countries, such as the USA, they are used to make an attractive boundary. The shingles are made from rot-resisting wood, and are similar to those sometimes used as roofing tiles on sheds and summerhouses.*

lower one. The effect is wall-like. Although a nice background for, say, trained fruit such as espaliers, shingle fences are generally unattractive on the other side, which is just the frame unless you go to the cost of cladding both sides. Perhaps worth considering for a distinctive internal divider or shelter, for example where the shingles match an adjoining summerhouse.

TRELLIS PANELS

Trellis panels are a serious proposition for boundaries between gardens, or perhaps where the garden backs onto open countryside. This is a good choice if you can link it with trellis panels within the garden, perhaps as internal dividers or simply as a decorative feature.

As a fence, however, they should be covered with climbers, as they are not attractive if left unclothed. Annual climbers such as the variegated Japanese hop (*Humulus japonicus* 'Variegatus') will give quick and almost complete cover by the end of the season, but it's best to have a little patience and plant perennials. If you want winter cover, the choice of climbers is quite limited – there are plenty of ivies, but among the flowering evergreens you are limited to plants such as evergreen honeysuckles (*Lonicera japonica* 'Halliana' and *L. henryi* for instance), though these are not a patch on the more common deciduous honeysuckles for flower power and fragrance.

Trellis panels that you plan to clothe with climbers need to be about 1.8 m (6 ft) tall.

WATTLE

Hazel wattle fences are seldom used nowadays, but they represent a traditional country craft. Similar fences known as osier hurdles are made from willow, but these are generally much more expensive. In each case, thin shoots are woven between upright stakes. You can buy panels 1.8 m (6 ft) long, and they are easy to secure by driving the stakes into the ground. Provide additional support with 7.5 cm (3 in) round posts and tie the panels to these with galvanized wire.

This kind of panel does not have a very long life, but is unobtrusive and 'sympathetic' in a garden setting. The panels are useful as an internal screen, perhaps for a compost heap or a fuel tank. They are also useful if you have had to cut back into an old hedge and need security while it regrows – the hedge will gradually grow through the wattle or hurdle.

The panels can be turned 'green' by planting ivies at

Fig. 10 *This type of fence, sometimes described as rustic lattice, has an informal rural appeal that makes an attractive boundary marker between gardens.*

the base – they will grow through the woven shoots from which the panels are made and provide an evergreen panel much narrower than a hedge.

RUSTIC LATTICE

This loose term covers those fences that use half-round poles nailed to horizontal bars in a criss-cross fashion to create a diamond or lattice pattern (Fig. 10). They can be made from scratch, but you will find it difficult to saw or obtain half-round poles. Usually they are bought as kits, and manufacturers may call this type of fence by different names, such as 'cottage' fence.

Rustic lattice is useful where you want an informal but decorative division between two properties.

CHAPTER 3

ERECTING A FENCE

Erecting a fence is well within the scope of most house-holders with even modest diy skills. The worst part of erecting a fence used to be making the post holes, but even this chore has been made easier with post spikes. This chapter shows just how easy it is.

HOW DEEP?

Use Table 1 as a guide to post sizes, if you are fixing the fence conventionally. If using a post spike, you will be able to save the length suggested for below ground (the saving on this will contribute towards the cost of this spike if you opt for that method).

For just one or two posts, simple spadework is probably the answer, but if you have many holes to dig it is worth hiring a post-hole borer (also described as post-hole augers). Inexpensive to hire, these have a corkscrew-like boring end and a large T-shaped handle at the top for leverage. Twisting the tool drives it into the earth. Pull it out of the hole after every 15 cm (6 in) or so, to remove the soil. If you hit very hard ground or rock it may be necessary to resort to other methods, but on most soils this is a quick and easy way to make post holes.

Make the hole a little deeper than required, and pack some hardcore (broken bricks or small stones) in the base to bring it to the correct level.

It is vital that the post is vertical, so enlist someone to

TABLE 1. CHOOSING THE RIGHT POST SIZE

Height of fence	Below ground	Post length	Post Dimension
0.6 m (2 ft)	0.3 m (1 ft)	0.9 m (3 ft)	63×75 mm (2½×3 in)
0.9 m (3 ft)	0.45 m (1½ ft)	1.35 m (4½ ft)	75×75 mm (3×3 in)
1.2 m (4 ft)	0.6 m (2 ft)	1.8 m (6 ft)	75×75 mm (3×3 in)
1.5 m (5 ft)	0.75 m (2½ ft)	2.25 m (7½ ft)	75×100 mm (3×4 in)
1.8 m (6 ft)	0.75 m (2½ ft)	2.55 m (8½ ft)	100×100 mm (4×4 in)
2.1 m (7 ft)	0.75 m (2½ ft)	2.85 m (9½ ft)	100×125 mm (4×5 in)

help by holding the post upright and checking verticals with a long spirit-level held against it, while you fix two or three battens to brace it into position. Nail the battens to the post and to stakes driven into the ground. If you are fixing a concrete post you will have to secure it with guy ropes instead.

Ram more hardcore around the post to wedge it firmly into the hole, leaving the top 30 cm (1 ft) for topping with concrete. Keep using the spirit-level to check that the post remains vertical – it is easy to push it out of alignment when ramming in hardcore.

Do not concrete all the posts at once unless you are sure the spacing is absolutely accurate – it is advisable to concrete them in after a few panels have been erected if fixing a panel fence; in the case of a closeboard fence it is usually done once the run or posts and arris rails have been fixed and secured in the correct position with hardcore or rubble.

For one or two posts, small bags of dry-mixed concrete is the most convenient option, but for a number of posts it is necessary to mix your own. Use 1 part cement to 2 parts of sand and 3 of aggregate. Using a stiff mix, tamp the concrete into the hole and finish off at the top with a slight slope or shoulder to help throw water away from the post. If possible, leave any struts in position for about a week to allow the concrete to set thoroughly, though you may have to reposition them to allow for the panels or fence to be fixed as you proceed.

FENCE-POST SPIKES

Fence-post spikes do not eliminate the hard work completely, but they do save digging holes. How easy they are to drive in depends very much on your ground: on stony or shallow soil over rock you will still have to resort to spade and pick-axe. But where the ground is suitable they are quick and relatively easy to use, with no bracing required and no mixing of concrete to worry about.

The spikes come in several sizes – for fences up to 1.2 m (4 ft) use a 60 cm (2 ft) spike; a 75 cm (2½ ft) one should be used for fences up to 1.8 m (6 ft) high (Fig. 11).

Don't try to drive the post straight into the ground by hitting the top of the spike with a sledgehammer; insert a short piece of hardwood into the post slot (or better still use the special metal insert or driving tool that you can buy from the fence supplier) and drive the post in by hitting this. This protects the spike itself. Use a heavy hammer or sledgehammer with slow, firm strokes to drive it into the ground vertically. Check at regular intervals with a spirit-level (slot a post in to check this, as it may not be possible to do it accurately by holding the level against the spike itself). If it begins to go a bit off course, use a crowbar to adjust it, then carry on.

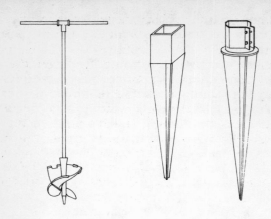

Fig. 11 *Fencing spikes can make erecting a fence even easier – instead of digging a hole you simply drive the stake into the ground. Some types can be tightened around the post once in position.*

Continue to drive the spike in until the socket is at ground level, then insert the post. The method of securing it will depend on the make – they are usually secured by screwing through pre-drilled holes in the socket, or by tightening a couple of clamping bolts.

Make sure that you buy posts to match the dimensions of the socket, even if this means deviating from the recommended sizes suggested on page 34.

You can also buy metal sockets for setting in concrete if this is more appropriate.

CONCRETE POSTS

Concrete posts will not rot in the ground but they may still blow over in a gale if not firmly anchored.

Concrete posts can look quite smart in the right situation – with panel fencing, for instance. They are sometimes used for chain link fences (special concrete struts are required for the end and corner posts), but they tend to be a bit too 'visible' with this kind of fence.

Concrete posts need to be ordered carefully. Unlike wooden posts, you can't simply nail the fence to the support. For panel fences you require posts with slots on each side, and different posts will be required for ends and corners; others suitable for fencing panels have a recess and special fixing brackets (this makes it easier to replace a panel as you don't have to slide it out vertically – not easy with a tall fence). Some posts, suitable for other kinds of fence, are pre-drilled or mortised, so seek the advice of the supplier.

HOW TO ERECT A PANEL FENCE

1. Work out the required height of the posts accurately, allowing a little above the height of the fence if you are adding a fence cap (desirable, though you can simply cut the top of the post at an angle to shed the water). It is a good idea to fix a gravel board – a strip of wood 15–23 cm (6–9 in) deep at the base of the fence – to keep the base of the panel out of contact with the ground. If fixing a gravel board, allow extra post height for this. Fix the first post as described on page 34, and lay a string line along the run of the fence so that subsequent posts are kept in line.

2. Fix the first panel before inserting the next post (panels and posts are done alternately), although you should excavate the holes ahead of the panels as it is difficult to make a hole with the panel in position (if using a fence spike, use the end of a fixed panel to position the next one). Support the panel on bricks and timber so that it is at the correct height, and have a helper hold it steady. Use a spirit-level on top of the panel to ensure that it is absolutely level.

Fig. 12 *Panel fences are quick and easy to erect, but make sure they are straight and level.*

3. Skew-nail the panel to the post with about three nails evenly spaced along the edge: If possible, do the same from the other side. Alternatively you can use metal brackets fixed to the post, in which case you can simply screw the panel to the bracket. These are inexpensive and available from most garden centres and fencing suppliers. Drill small holes first to take the screws.

4. Fit the gravel board if being used (advisable). The simplest way of doing this is with a bracket – either like the ones for fixing the main panels, or special gravel board brackets that you can buy.

5. Position the next post, packing it with hardcore to hold the post in the correct vertical position as a helper checks with a spirit-level.

6. Saw the tops of the posts to an even height, and nail on the caps.

HOW TO ERECT A CLOSEBOARD FENCE

1. Start by stretching a line along the course of the fence so that it is erected in a straight line. Then excavate the first post hole (see page 33). Generally closeboard fencing posts are cut to a slope at the top, so you do not need to allow additional length for capping, but you do need to allow for a gravel board.

2. Position the first post, ramming it into an upright position with hardcore. If you have not been able to buy posts with the mortises already cut (concrete and some wooden posts are mortised when you buy them), you will have to remove them yourself. Mark out and cut 50 mm × 22 mm (2 in × ⅞ in) mortises about 15 cm (6 in) below the top of the post and the same distance above the gravel board level. If the fence is no more than 1.2 m (4 ft) high that is adequate, but taller fences require an additional mortise half way between the others. The mortise should be about 2.5 cm (1 in) in from the front of the post (the side to which the feather-edged boards will be nailed).

3. Shape the ends of the arris rails, which are roughly triangular in profile, so that they fit the mortises. A coarse rasp or file will be useful for final fitting. Paint the prepared ends thoroughly with a wood preservative.

4. Prepare the next hole, which should be no more than 3 m (10 ft) away, and leave the post loose in it at

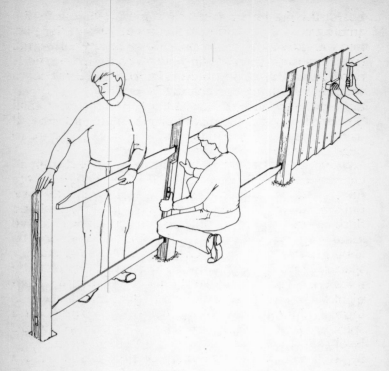

Fig. 13 *Closeboard fencing requires more patience to erect but is still a relatively simple d-i-y job. Use a spacer guide to ensure the feather-edged boards are evenly spaced.*

this stage. Then insert the arris rails in the first post and, with a helper, raise the second post into position, slotting the arris rails into it. Ram hardcore around the post to keep it upright once the rails have been checked again with a spirit-level.

5. Continue until all the posts and arris rails are in position (if using concrete posts mortised for a gravel board, this has to be inserted at the same time as the arris rails, as you proceed), then nail through the post into the tenon and finally pack the holes with concrete (see pages 34–5), checking horizontals and verticals once again with a spirit-level. If possible, leave for a week before fixing the boards.

6. Fix the gravel board by nailing through cleats (small blocks of wood), into both gravel board and post. If using concrete posts without mortises, nail the board to pegs driven into the ground.

7. Cut the feather-edged boards to length, and paint all cut surfaces with a preservative. Rest the bottom of the first board on the gravel board, and nail into the arris rail through the thick part of the board, which should be flush against the post. Position the next board in the same way, but this time overlapping the first one by about 12 mm (½ in). To ensure even spacing, make a spacer from a scrap of wood. Drive the nails through the thick edge again, but avoid the nail going through both planks. The last board fixed will require additional nails through the thin edge of the board too. Check with a spirit-level occasionally to ensure that the boards are level (Fig. 13).

8. It is a good idea, although not essential, to add a capping strip along the top of the fence, as it looks more finished and will help to shed rain. Always treat the whole fence (both sides!) with a good wood preservative.

Note: If you do not want to cut mortises you could secure the arris rails with brackets sold for arris rail repairs, but they can mar the appearance of the fence.

PRESERVING YOUR INVESTMENT

All timber for garden fences requires preservative treatment, and some woods more than others. You may be fortunate enough to buy wood with a natural rot resistance – oak posts or cedar shingles for instance – but even these will benefit in appearance if treated with a wood preservative periodically. Most fencing timber is likely to be a relatively cheap wood, however, and you will have to put more effort into preserving your investment. Always try to buy pre-treated posts: they will cost more but you simply can't protect the timber beneath ground once the post is inserted, and those preservatives that you paint on do not penetrate the wood to the same extent as pressure-treated or vacuum-treated timber.

Creosote is the most popular paint-on wood preservative for fences. Fresh creosote will harm plants, especially if splashed on the leaves, but once dry it is unlikely to cause any harm to plants outdoors.

If you prefer not to use creosote, there are products harmless to plants and with a less unpleasant smell. Some of these are more like stains that contain a preservative, and these may not be so effective unless you apply them regularly, perhaps as a top-up to initial treatment with a more potent preservative.

There are many types and makes of preservative, and a large d-i-y store will stock a good range. Check the instructions on the tin and simply choose one that best suits you and the job in hand – you may want one that won't do too much harm if you splash it on plants, for instance; or you may decide to choose one that does not have a pungent smell.

Always read the instructions carefully: it is usually advisable to wear protective gloves and goggles and to avoid breathing the vapour if possible. However, once applied and dry preservative should be safe. Some can be sprayed onto the fence, but there is more risk from drift than with painting it on.

Be prepared to apply two coats initially, and pay special attention to end-grain and cut surfaces.

Painting on a preservative is not really adequate for timber in contact with the ground – it should really be soaked in the preservative, overnight if possible. Post ends can usually be immersed in a bucket or tub containing the preservative, but for longer timbers (such as gravel boards) you can improvise a trough from a sheet of thick polythene draped over loose bricks (to form the edges). Place a few bricks on top of the timbers to keep them immersed. When you have finished, carefully return the unused preservative to a suitable container, for use on the rest of the fence.

You can buy special preservative pellets to insert into drill holes in order to arrest timber decay; it may be worth inserting a couple of these at the bottom of your posts.

Re-apply a preservative every year or two – be guided by the manufacturer's recommendations as some require more frequent applications than others.

REPAIRS

There comes a point at which all fences require some kind of repair, no matter how conscientious you have been with the preservative. An exceptional gale may find a weak point, even though the rest of the fence is perfectly sound. Prompt repairs can put off more expensive bills later.

LOOSE FEATHER-EDGED BOARDS

The feather-edged boards used for closeboard fencing may tend to work loose with the shrinking and expansion of the timber over time. Often gales loosen the nails. Remove the old nails completely, and if the board is in good condition simply renail – avoiding the position of the old nails. If the board is in poor

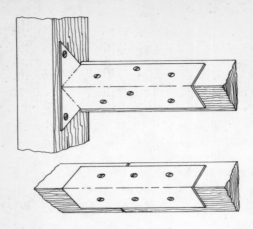

Fig. 14 *With time arris rails on closeboard fences tend to rot or break. They are easily repaired with metal brackets.*

condition, buy a new one (these are sometimes sold by large d-i-y stores as well as fencing suppliers), slide it in and fix with rust-proof nails.

ROTTEN ARRIS RAIL

Sometimes the arris rail is one of the first parts to fail on a closeboard fence – they tend to rot near the tenon. Simply buy a galvanized metal support bracket to screw on: cheap, simple, and effective. They are widely available in garden centres and large d-i-y stores as well as from fencing suppliers.

Occasionally an arris rail may rot or snap along its length, and simple reinforcing brackets are available for this eventuality (Fig. 14).

GRAVEL BOARDS

Gravel boards are intended to be replaced easily. Excavate a shallow trench along the base of the fence to make the job easier. If the original board was fixed with cleats or to pegs, simply remove these and replace at the same time as the fresh board. If the board was fixed into slots or brackets, saw through the old board at the ends, and fix the new one with pegs driven into the ground (you will not be able to use the old fixings).

REPLACING A PANEL

Fence panels usually come in standard sizes and are easily replaced. If slotted concrete posts are used, the old one can be removed and a new one slotted in; those fixed with metal brackets can simply be unscrewed and the panel replaced. If you have to buy a panel that does not quite fit, a wooden infill piece can usually be fixed to the side to make up small differences.

REPLACING A POST

The simplest way to repair a wooden post that has broken at the base is to bolt a concrete spur to it. These are widely available from fencing suppliers, builders' merchants and some large d-i-y stores.

The hardest part is excavating a hole by the side of the old post, especially if it has been set in concrete. You will probably have to chisel it away with a club hammer and cold chisel – if you have many to do it may be worth hiring a power tool for breaking up concrete.

It may be necessary to support the fence by bracing it with wooden battens while repairing the post.

Saw any rotten area off the base of the post and treat the surface with a preservative, then insert the concrete spur in a hole 45–60 cm (18–24 in) deep, making sure it is flush against the post.

Push the bolts provided through the pre-drilled holes, and knock them with a hammer so that they leave a mark on the wood. Remove the spur and drill holes through the post. Then replace the spur and bolt it to the post.

Saw off any protruding bolt to make a neater job, then set the spur in concrete, using a spirt-level to check that the post is vertical.

CHAPTER 4

GATES

Garden gates are less popular than they were in the first half of the century, partly as a result of the less enclosed design of many modern gardens but also because they have become less fashionable. A gate is a necessary part of any fence, however, and if you must rely on the gate to provide security for pets and children it may be better to position it at the side of the house to partition off the back garden. Casual visitors to the front door will not always shut the gate so it's best not to take risks.

MAKING AN ENTRANCE

Gates at the side of the house are usually practical, but you can make them ornamental too, perhaps by framing them with a brick arch. This kind of device makes you want to go through the arch to explore, and framing a gate always makes it more of a feature.

Suppliers' catalogues may group gates according to position or use: *side gates* are generally strong and relatively plain, being intended for security; *entrance gates* are usually more decorative and may be lighter in construction though they must be strong enough for frequent use; *drive gates* are obviously wider, and may be designed in two sections rather than one very wide swing.

With the exception of drive gates, do not be too influenced by labels – it's more important to buy a gate that looks right for the situation and blends with the fence, wall or hedge. If you have a picket fence, an open picket-style gate is appropriate; most panel fence manufacturers produce panel gates that will match in height and style.

It is especially important to think about gates at an early stage if building a wall, which we will be looking at in Chapter 5. You need to leave the correct space for the gate when you construct the wall, so it's a good idea to buy the gate beforehand; you can then also incorporate the gate hinges and fixings as you build the piers.

Before ordering any gate, however, make sure that it will actually open in the way intended without obstructions, such as higher ground or a path edging. Decide also on its minimum width – maybe you want to allow plenty of space to use a wheelbarrow or a wheelchair, for instance.

BUYING GATES

You can buy gates from some large d-i-y stores, some garden centres (probably a limited range), and builders' merchants. However, it is probably worth sending away for some catalogues from specialist manufacturers, if only to know what's available. They often advertise in gardening, d-i-y and lifestyle magazines.

Make sure you order the correct hinges and fasteners at the same time. Flush-fitting gates are aligned with the back of the posts, a method usually used for single timber gates, using tee-hinges or strap hinges. Centred hinges are usually used for metal gates and are likely to be of the pin type (as the name implies these are fixed to the centre of the post or recess). Back-hanging gates, which are fitted behind the posts, only open inwards but will shut against the post if required; these are sometimes used for wide single gates or double gates. If in doubt, explain your requirements to the supplier.

MATERIALS

Timber gates

These are available in hardwoods and softwoods. You pay much more for the former, but if you can afford it they are a much better buy as they are considerably more durable. Softwood gates are an acceptable compromise if you can't afford the hardwood versions and are prepared to keep them well preserved or painted.

Metal gates

More appropriate in some settings, but avoid very elaborate wrought-iron gates in a modest setting, otherwise they will look pretentious. Wrought iron and aluminium are both used for gates; the wrought iron may rust if not properly protected, as many are actually made from mild steel bar which must be primed and painted.

Posts

These can be steel tube, concrete or timber – the latter is by far the most popular and most readily available. If fixing to a wall, you can usually anchor the gate straight to the masonry piers. If buying concrete posts, make sure they are pre-drilled for suitable fittings; ordinary fence posts are unsuitable.

HOW TO HANG A GATE

TO REPLACE AN OLD GATE BETWEEN EXISTING SUPPORTS

You may only have to make sure you order a new gate of the right size, though it may be necessary to ensure that hinges and latches are placed in a new position to ensure they are fixed firmly. Most gates are manufactured to a range of fairly standard widths, but it may be necessary to shop around; some manufacturers will make a gate to fit a particular opening. If the gap is only a little too wide for a standard off-the-shelf gate, it may be possible to add a strip of timber onto the gate posts; if it is too wide for this, move one of the posts closer.

TO HANG A GATE FROM SCRATCH

Using timber posts, lay the gate and posts on the ground, placing them so that the posts, gate and fittings are all accurately spaced. Then nail battens to the gate posts, to keep them at the correct spacing (crucial if you are to avoid problems later). Nail one across near the top of the posts, another near the bottom, but above what will be ground level, and a third diagonally between the first two (Fig. 15).

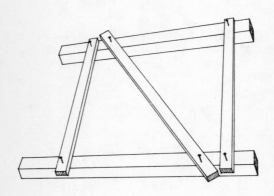

Fig. 15 *To ensure that the posts are correctly spaced for a gate, nail battens between them to hold the posts the correct distance apart before inserting in their prepared holes.*

Make sure the posts are preservative treated.

Excavate the post holes, making them about 7.5 cm (3 in) deeper than the amount of post to be buried, and place a brick in the bottom of each hole for the posts to rest on. At least 45 cm (1½ ft) of post should be below ground for a low gate; at least 60 cm (2 ft) for a tall one.

Lower the braced posts into position and check for clearances (add hardcore beneath the bricks if the gate has to be raised). Check levels and verticals with a spirit-level, then pack hardcore round the posts before again using the spirit-level and filling the holes with a concrete mix (1 part cement, 1 part sand, 3 parts aggregate). If the posts seem in the least unstable, fix battens nailed to pegs in the ground to hold them firmly in position. Wait a week before adding the fittings and hanging the gate.

CHAPTER 5

WALLS

Walled gardens are the dream of many gardeners, but of course the type of garden wall that most of us are able to consider building may be far removed from the large enclosing walls of the traditional walled kitchen garden. Expense alone is prohibitive, but the work involved in creating high walls would deter all but the most enthusiastic d-i-y bricklayer; and in a small modern garden, high walls would in any case be oppressive.

Most garden walls are modest affairs, intended as no-maintenance boundary markers more than enclosures, but by combining them with hedges or even a trellis, it is possible to create practical barriers and a high degree of privacy too, even with a low wall. A low wall backed by a taller hedge provides an effective barrier close to the ground (where hedges are often vulnerable), and the contrast between the hard landscaping of the wall and the natural beauty of a living hedge can be striking from a design point of view.

Concrete screen block walls are easy to erect to a height of about 1.8 m (6 ft) even with very basic skills, and although these do not provide a lot of shelter and privacy on their own, they are useful as a screen for a patio, especially used in conjunction with shrubs planted in front. And they can be used to good effect for a boundary wall too, perhaps combined with bricks.

Mixing materials can be very effective, and can prevent a wall becoming oppressive in a small garden.

Wooden fencing panels on a low brick wall can provide height while still retaining the impression of something more secure and distinctive than wooden fencing alone. Screen blocks integrated into a low brick wall will add a touch of distinction and a stronger sense of design. And both screen blocks introduced into a brick wall, and a brick or concrete low wall combined with a hedge or a dense planting of shrubs, will be much more efficient at filtering wind than a solid wall or fence. A solid screen simply causes turbulence within the garden, whereas something that filters it and breaks its force will often provide more protection.

For the really ambitious, brick walls can be used as key design features, creating 'windows' in them through which a particular view of the garden, or a vista outside, can be viewed within the frame. Professionals can create circular 'windows', but even a rectangular one is ambitious for an amateur. If you are having the wall laid for you, however, it is worth considering this kind of feature, which will transform an otherwise boring tall wall into a truly distinguished one.

BRICKS AND BLOCKS

Brick walls are usually the most suitable for brick-built houses, though if the house wall is rendered and perhaps painted a pale colour, screen blocks can look very appropriate. A stone or imitation stone wall may look best for a stone-built house. It is always worth trying to integrate the garden wall with the materials used in the home to create a strong sense of design.

Bricks

These come in many shades and textures and it is often possible to buy them to match the house brick closely. They require much care when buying, however, as many bricks are unsuitable for garden walls, even though they may have been used for the home. Bricks that are perfectly able to withstand the surface wetting from just the exposed side may not be able to resist the effect of thorough wetting from both sides and then freezing, as they begin to split and flake.

Bricks suitable for garden walls (and for paving) may be described as 'special quality', but do check that they are suitable for the purpose intended. Not all builders' suppliers are knowledgeable about the qualities of the bricks that they sell, so if in doubt about suitability, find out the name of the manufacturer and seek his advice.

As an approximate guide to quantities, for a wall a single brick wide (technically a 'half-brick' wall) you will require 60 bricks for each square metre. For a 'full-brick' wall (two bricks wide), 120 will be required.

Concrete block walling

Much more variable in both sizes and colours, but at least you know that all concrete blocks are suitable for walls. Some blocks, however, are more suitable for raised beds than boundary walls (especially those with only one good 'face'). The easiest walling blocks to work with are those of fairly modest size, and more or less brick shaped. These can be laid like ordinary bricks. Most manufacturers also produce blocks in various sizes to enable you to create a random effect; these can look especially effective in a rural setting, particularly where natural stone walls are widespread, but they require considerable planning and skill to construct well.

Concrete walling blocks, resembling natural stone, and sometimes available in rather unnatural colours, are widely available from builders' merchants and some garden centres. A number of manufacturers produce very good catalogues, and these usually illustrate constructed walls, which will enable you to visualize the finished wall more easily, but you will probably have to buy from a local stockist.

Screen block walling

Comparatively easy to construct. As the alternative name of pierced block walling implies, these rectangular blocks have a pattern with 'holes' that you can see through, producing a decorative effect. They are more widely used as internal screens or partitions within the garden (often to define a patio area), but can be used for a boundary wall.

Screen blocks are stacked, one above the other, rather than bonded like bricks, and being much larger than bricks, the wall will go up relatively quickly.

It is not easy to visualize the final wall from individual screen blocks, so try to see an area of constructed wall, or judge from pictures in catalogues. The finished appearance of the wall can look very different from one pattern to another, even though the block sizes are identical. Think about colour too. Some are a much purer white than others – useful if you want to create a very bold, almost Mediterranean look. For many situations, however, perhaps where you do not want to draw attention to the wall as a feature, the normal off-white or buff colour may be more appropriate.

A small wall is generally constructed from blocks of the same pattern, but a fairly large area of screen walling benefits from a few different blocks interspersed here and there (randomly or to a pattern). Use a solid block, maybe with a similar embossed pattern to the pierced blocks, rather than a totally different pierced block (unless you use a pattern that is self-contained; in other words one that does not require adjoining blocks to form a larger overall pattern). Always choose these variation blocks from the same manufacturer as the main walling blocks, otherwise the colour or texture may vary and the 'odd' block will jar rather than look part of an intentional design.

Although screen block walls can be built straight onto a concrete foundation, a tall pierced block wall may look better if built onto a low concrete block wall. By choosing walling blocks that match the paving, and integrating the screen blocks with this low wall, the whole area will look more designed and integrated. Top the walling blocks with matching coping, and build the screen block wall on these.

BUYING BRICKS AND BLOCKS

A good builders' merchant specializing in garden stonework is likely to offer the widest selection of walling blocks and probably a good range of bricks too. General builders' merchants usually stock a reasonable range of bricks (though you cannot assume that the staff are competent to advise on their suitability for particular jobs), and a limited range of walling blocks.

Large d-i-y stores sometimes stock both bricks and walling blocks, but generally the range is very limited.

If you require a large quantity of bricks it may be worth contacting local brick manufacturers. This can be a good way to buy bricks relatively cheaply if they will supply you, but to make the delivery economic, you are normally expected to take a large quantity.

Garden centres may sell a range of walling blocks, and a few sell bricks, but the selection is unlikely to be as good as that at a large builders' merchant.

FIRM FOUNDATIONS

All walls, even low ones, require a concrete foundation for stability and safety; you can, however, lay a low wall directly onto paving stones provided the paving has itself been laid on proper foundations.

Tall brick or block walls (other than screen blocks) require more than elementary d-i-y expertise and are beyond the scope of this book; and supporting walls also require additional know-how and more stringent foundations and reinforcements. Low garden walls should present few problems, however, and the following advice should be adequate.

'Setting out' is the term used to describe the job of marking out and excavating the area for the foundations. The width of the foundation should be about three times the width of the wall, though for a low wall perhaps only 60 cm (2 ft) high, you may get away with twice the width. For a wall only a single brick or block wide (a single skin or half-brick wall), 13 cm (5 in) of hardcore and 15 cm (6 in) of concrete is generally adequate; for a wall with two bricks or blocks side by side (a double skin or full-brick wall), this should be increased to about 23 cm (9 in) of concrete over 13 cm (5 in) of hardcore.

Excavate the trench to leave the finished 'footing' about 15 cm (6 in) below ground level for a single skin (half-brick) wall, or 23 cm (9 in) for a double skin (full-brick) wall.

Ram hardcore (broken bricks and rubble) in the base of the trench to provide a firm base, and top with a concrete mix of 1 part cement to 5 parts combined aggregate (or 1 part cement, 2½ parts sharp sand, 3½ parts 20 mm aggregate), tamping it to compact and level it. Allow it to stand for a week to harden, before laying the bricks or blocks.

HOW TO BUILD A WALL

Although the term 'brick' is used here, the same principles apply to concrete block walls, although the variation in size may require modification; and if building a wall with blocks of different sizes, to produce a random stone effect, it may not be possible to use the bonding patterns illustrated (Fig. 16). The instructions below are for a single skin wall; for a double skin wall lay the two rows at once, and add wall ties (obtainable from a builders' merchant) to secure the rows together if the bond does not have bricks running cross-ways through the wall to tie the leaves of the wall together.

1. Lay a line fixed between pegs to work against and ensure a straight line. Then using a bricklayer's trowel place a ridge of mortar on the concrete footing. Draw the trowel toward you, releasing a slice of mortar as you do so. Use the edge of the trowel to spread it over the surface in a wave-like motion, in a layer about 12 mm (½ in) thick.

2. Lay a row of bricks along the line, starting at a corner. Butter one end of the next brick with mortar, and butt that against the previous one. Tap each brick down on to the mortar bed with the handle of the trowel.

3. Check levels with a spirit-level after every few bricks, then after any adjustments strike off surplus mortar from the joints.

4. Build up the corners first, to about three or four courses, then stretch a line between the ends as a level guide for laying the intermediate bricks. Once the first course has been laid, it is important to check the wall frequently for vertical as well as horizontal accuracy.

5. Strengthening piers (free-standing masonry columns) will be required every 2.4 m (8 ft) or so, especially on a single skin wall. The best spacing will depend on the height of the wall.

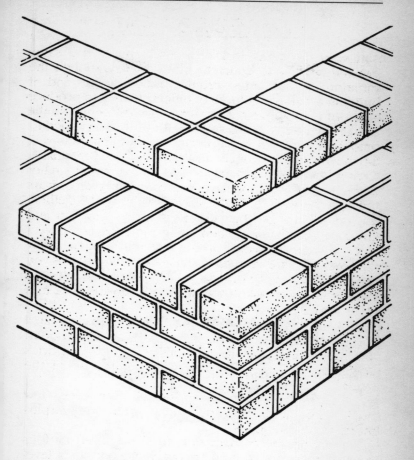

Fig. 16 *For a simple brick wall just one brick thick, a stretcher bond (upper) is the best choice, but even for low walls strengthening piers may be necessary.*

This English garden wall bond (lower) is stronger for a taller wall, but obviously requires more bricks. At the corners it is necessary to cut a brick in half lengthways, but this is easy with a little practice.

6. An hour or two after a section of brickwork has been laid and the mortar has begun to harden, point the wall.

For a recessed joint, use a round metal bar or pipe about 10 mm across, bent sufficiently to provide a handle that will hold your knuckles clear of the brickwork. Simply smooth the joints with this. Other methods of pointing can be used, but this is a quick and simple method for beginners. You should be able to remove mortar splashes from the face of the bricks with a stiff brush once it has started to dry.

MORTAR MIXES

For a very small wall the convenience of ready-mixed dry pack mortar (from d-i-y stores) may be worth the higher cost. For a lot of bricklaying, it is cheaper and more practical to mix your own.

FOR GENERAL BRICK AND BLOCK LAYING

Mix 1 part cement, 1½ parts lime and 6 parts soft (builder's) sand. Alternatively, use 1 part masonry cement to 5 parts soft sand (no lime is then required if masonry cement is used).

FOR COURSES BELOW GROUND LEVEL

Mix 1 part cement, 1½ parts lime and 4 parts soft sand. Alternatively use 1 part masonry cement to 3 part soft sand.

Only mix enough mortar for about half an hour's work, with a consistency that is thick enough to compress to about 12 mm (½ in) when you gently press a brick onto a ribbon of it.

HOW TO BUILD A SCREEN BLOCK WALL

Screen block walls are constructed on a totally different principle from brick walls. They are stacked rather than bonded like bricks, so special pilaster columns are used to provide the necessary strength and rigidity. These will require reinforcing on all except low walls. As intermediate pilasters have slots in two opposite sides, corner ones in two adjacent sides, and end pilasters only in one side, it is important to calculate accurately the number of each type required. Pilasters are required at intervals of ten blocks (3 m, 10 ft). Coping blocks are required to finish off and protect the screen blocks, and pier caps to top the pilasters. Never try to save money by omitting these – they help to protect the wall but also give it a more finished appearance (Fig. 17).

1. Always start from a firm footing. If not laying on paving already bedded on firm foundations, prepare a base as described for brick walls (see page 57). Make the footing twice the width of the pilaster blocks. Walls over 1.5 m (5 ft) high will require steel reinforcing rods for the pilasters and these should be embedded into the wall footing. It may be necessary to keep them upright with guy ropes until the concrete has set. Always calculate the spacing for these rods very accurately: lay out a row of blocks and pilasters loosely on the ground alongside the footing, allowing for 12 mm (½ in) mortar joints, so that the rods can be calculated to run up the centre of the pilasters when they are positioned. Reinforcement is not essential for lower walls.

2. Once the footing has cured for about a week, fix a line to work to, then mortar the first end pilaster block into position (if reinforcing rods are used, it will be necessary to pass the block over the rod). Make sure the slot is facing in the right direction. Mortar a second and third pilaster block in position. Check with a spirit-level that the blocks are vertical as well as horizontal.

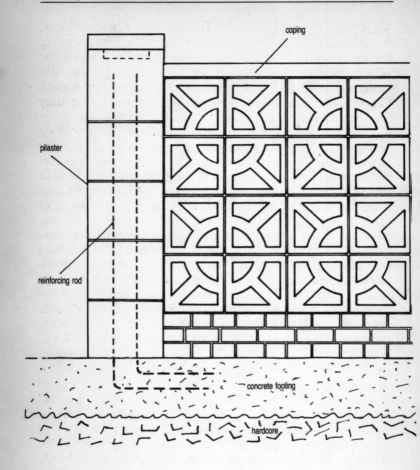

coping

pilaster

reinforcing rod

concrete footing

hardcore

Fig. 17 *Screen or pierced block walls are ideal for patios or as internal dividers within the garden, and are the easiest kind of wall for the beginner to contemplate. There are many different block designs, one of which is illustrated.*

3. Erect the next pilaster column in the same way, having spaced the intermediate blocks loosely, allowing for mortar joints (it will not be necessary to lay out the blocks like this if reinforcing rods were set in the concrete, as it will have been done at an earlier stage). Construct all the pilaster piers in this way so that they are three blocks high.

4. Mark a line on the footing to lay the intermediate blocks to – as these are inset from the edge of the pilasters it may be difficult to use string, but you can draw a chalk line. Lay a bed of mortar along the line of the wall, but only sufficient for, say, five blocks at one time. Fit the first block by buttering a vertical edge with mortar, being careful to keep it off the face of the block, and bed it into position into the groove in the first pilaster. Butter one vertical edge on the next block and butt that up to the first, using a spirit-level to check horizontals and verticals, and tapping them into position with the handle of the trowel if necessary. It will be helpful to have the row of blocks laid out loosely alongside, so that you can confirm that the spacing between each block is about right, and that you will not have difficulty fitting in the last block, which will have to be buttered with mortar on two vertical edges.

5. Once the first row of blocks has been laid accurately, the rest is relatively simple. Add the second row of block, bedding them on a ridge of mortar laid on top of the first row – the two rows of screen blocks will then bring the wall level with the three pilaster blocks. If using reinforcing rods, make sure these are firmly fixed by packing mortar or concrete into the hollow core of the pilasters, around the steel rods. Repeat this as you proceed.

6. Press reinforcement wire mesh or a strip of folded wire-netting into the mortar bed before adding the next three pilaster blocks and two rows of screen blocks. Repeat this horizontal reinforcement for every second row of screen blocks. A concave joint (see brick walls) is generally the most visually pleasing for screen block walls, but you can remove a little mortar from the joints before it sets and point it with another finish; and even use a coloured mortar if you want a distinctive or contrasting finish.

7. Mortar the coping pieces and wall caps into position.

BLOCKS WITH BRICKS

Screen blocks can be integrated with bricks, with the brickwork forming a low base perhaps six to eight courses high, and the brick pillars being extended to the height of the wall. The pillars should have a reinforcing rod mortared into the centre.

It is important to make the brick piers correspond with the level of the screen blocks. Four courses of brick (including the mortar joints) should bring the piers to the same height as one screen block.

Fix the screen blocks as the brick piers are built, so that the reinforcing wire mesh can bridge the blocks and every fourth course of bricks.

Take the coping straight across the top of both screen blocks and brick piers, so that it provides a neat finish and also helps to provide an additional tie between the two.

DRY STONE WALLS

Natural stone walls can be particularly attractive in rural areas, but they can look out of place in a town setting or on a housing estate. The advantage is that you can plant suitable alpines into the face of the wall in a way that is never convincing with other types of wall, even if some mortar is removed and replaced with soil to provide a root-hold. Dry stone walls are not a cheap option, however, unless you happen to live in an area where the stone occurs naturally and there is a local supplier.

Dry stone walls are difficult to build well unless you have experience, and few of us are likely to build enough of them to become really proficient; but for an internal division within the garden, perhaps separating one part of the garden off informally from another, or for a *low* boundary wall, it is worth having a try.

Excavate a shallow trench, so that the base of the wall starts below ground level, then use large, flat stones to provide a stable foundation for the rest of the wall. The base should always be wider than the top, with the sides sloping inwards by about 2.5 cm (1 in) for every 30 cm (1 ft) of height; so decide on the required width of the top and the height of the wall and calculate the base width accordingly. The height of the wall should not exceed its width at the base – bear in mind that gravity is going to hold the wall together, and stones should not be dislodged by ice forming and expanding in winter. Do not be too ambitious regarding height, and always make sure the 'batter' (slope) is maintained. To ensure this, a batter gauge can be made from three battens nailed together to give the appropriate angle (it is used by holding a spirit-level against the vertical side while the batter gauge is held against the wall.

It is unlikely that you will have many stones large enough to span the full width of the base, so lay two facing rows, sloping slightly inwards towards the centre. Infill spaces in the centre with small stones and rubble.

It is, however, important to introduce as many 'bondstones' as possible, which span the whole width, so try to introduce these periodically as the wall is built.

Once the first course has been laid, build up the ends, adjusting the position of the stones until they fit together with little or no movement. Use small stones or rubble to fill in any gaps. Tilt the stones inwards slightly (this will also help to create the 'batter', as well as general stability), and work from each end toward the centre.

Be sure to reserve some large, flat stones for the top course.

MORTARED NATURAL STONE WALLS

For a boundary wall that adjoins the public highway, a similar visual effect to a dry stone wall can be achieved with a mortared wall, but for an amateur it will produce a safer, more stable result.

The basic principles of the dry stone wall can be applied, but the batter need only be 2.5 cm (1 in) in 60 cm (2 ft), and the range of stone that can be used is greater. For a dry stone wall lots of large but fairly flat stones are required, but for a mortared wall it is possible to use smaller and more rectangular stones.

Lay the first course with the largest stones available, using string guidelines to keep the lines as straight as possible. Apply mortar to fill the joints completely, but find stones that fit as snugly as possible. Use small stones and extra mortar to fill any gaps in the centre of the wall.

Reserve some large flat stones for the top of the wall.

Point the joints before the mortar hardens, raking out the mortar about 12 mm (½ in) deep with a blunt pointed stick. Excess mortar can be brushed off the stones with a stiff brush.

CHAPTER 6

HEDGES

Hedges are the most labour-intensive of all boundary markers to maintain, and it can take years for them to become really effective as a screen or barrier. From a purely horticultural viewpoint, a hedge is always more appealing than a fence or wall, but bear in mind that a hedge will impoverish the soil so it will be difficult to plant close up to the base of it very successfully. You *can* successfully plant close to the base of a wall or fence, provided the ground is kept watered in dry weather.

Given these drawbacks one might wonder why so many hedges are planted. The answer is simple: they are generally much less expensive than fences and walls, are more efficient as a windbreak (they reduce the wind speed rather than causing turbulence and wind damage further back into the garden), and they will probably far outlive a wooden fence. But, above all, hedges are simply more appealing to most gardeners. They never look oppressive or ugly in the way that some walls and fences can if not constructed with thought, and many are very beautiful in flower or foliage.

For screening, hedges can sometimes be used where fences and walls might be forbidden. Restrictions in deeds and highway regulations might forbid a fence or wall above a certain height, but not apply to hedges.

Hedges can also contribute much to the sense of design. They can be castellated, or built up to form an arch over a gateway. Topiary can be introduced; they can be clipped formally or left informal. And great variety of texture and colour can be created by choosing suitable plants, perhaps mixing them within the same hedge to create a patchwork of colours such as greens and purples.

Although the majority of hedges are grown for foliage effect (evergreens are especially popular because they provide year-round cover and privacy), flowering hedges are a perfectly practical proposition. Berries can add another dimension to a hedge, and of course these may provide a longer-lasting display than flowers.

WHICH TYPE OF HEDGE

Anyone who has not given hedges much thought before may be surprised at the extensive range of plants that can be used. There really are hedges of all shapes and sizes, from dwarfs of 45 cm (1½ ft) or less, to huge hedges or screens more than 6 m (20 ft) tall. Some are dense and animal-proof, others more open but highly decorative. Some will need regular and frequent trimming, others will require no more than an annual trim; a few will grow so fast that they will be difficult to keep compact, others grow slowly and will never become a problem. There is certain to be a hedge that's suitable for a particular situation; choosing the right one is the key to whether you will find your hedge a pleasure or a pain.

It is impossible to select the best hedge for your needs unless priorities and requirements are clearly thought through first. Does it have to provide privacy? Does it have to be animal-proof? Should it be a deterrent barrier or simply a token boundary marker? Does it have to be low-maintenance, or are you prepared to trim regularly if necessary (powered tools can make relatively light work of this)? Is the hedge required to act as a screen? Which is more important, quick early growth or infrequent cutting later? Is a formal hedge required or an informal one? Does it have to be a decorative feature in its own right, or will it simply fulfil a practical purpose? Does it have to be evergreen, or are you prepared to sacrifice year-round cover for more variety and perhaps a more decorative hedge?

To make selection easier, the plants in this chapter have been divided into two main groups: formal hedges and informal hedges. These have been further divided into height ranges, but heights can only be a guide as much depends on how the hedge is pruned and trained in the formative years, and how well it is clipped later. A beech hedge can be kept to a height of 1.2 m (4 ft) quite easily, yet beech will also make a hedge twice this height if you want it that high – and if you adjust the spacing when planting, it is possible to double it again. A beech hedge over 26 m (85 ft) tall has been known, so do bear in mind that each plant will make a full-sized beech tree if left to grow naturally – it is only the spacing and pruning or trimming that makes the difference to height.

CUTTING DOWN ON THE TRIMMING

Hedge trimming is a tedious job, and it must be high on the list of unpopular garden tasks. It can be made easier, however, with a powered hedgetrimmer.

Hand shears are still useful for very small hedges or for intricate work like arches and topiary, but for a general run of hedge, a hedgetrimmer ranks with a powered lawnmower as a really useful labour-saving tool. They vary a lot in capabilities and ease of use, as well as price, so it is worth putting some thought into buying a hedgetrimmer.

The blade length will determine how quickly you can

cut a hedge, as the longer the blade the more quickly a given length of hedge will be cut. Unfortunately long blades can make the tool heavier and more tiring to use. A 400 mm blade is a good compromise for a small garden, but if you have a lot of hedge to cut a 600 mm blade may prove a better bet.

A double-sided blade (one that cuts on both sides) could save time if you cut on both sweeps, but you may find it easier to control if you cut in one direction only, so the benefits of double-sided blades may be offset if you are not used to handling this type of machine.

The blade action also affects how tiring you may find a hedgetrimmer to use. Reciprocating blades move against each other, and generally cause less vibration than those where one blade cuts against a stationary blade.

Teeth that are closely spaced are more likely to produce a smooth, even finish, but are most suitable for regularly trimmed hedges. A trimmer with widely spaced teeth will cope more easily with the thicker shoots of a more neglected or less frequently trimmed hedge.

Safety features to look for include blade extensions (to help prevent serious cuts if you have an accident), a blade brake (to stop the blades quickly), and a two-handed switch (so that you will not be tempted to use the tool one-handed).

A suitable hedgetrimmer that you find easy to use (usually a compromise between weight and blade length) can make light work of hedge trimming, and you may be prepared to consider those hedges that require cutting two or three times during the growing season if they fulfil your requirements for a good hedge in other respects.

A growth retardant can be used to reduce the amount of cutting required for many quick-growing hedges. A chemical called dikegulac (sold in the UK under the trade name Cutlass) regulates the growth of a hedge if you spray it thoroughly after a light trimming. Apply it on a still day during active growth (usually from late spring). A few shoots may grow out but are easily trimmed off; otherwise you can expect a fairly neat hedge for the rest of the season. It is suitable for most hedges, including privet, hawthorn, holly, berberis, laurel, beech, *Lonicera nitida*, Leyland cypress, and thuja. With a few hedges, special precautions may be necessary.

This type of product does not eliminate the work of keeping a hedge in trim: it still has to be cut once a year, and there is the task of spraying it thoroughly. For quick-growing hedges like privet and *Lonicera nitida*, however, you may consider it a good time-saver and worth the cost.

QUICK SCREENS

The ideal hedge for screening would be one that grows very rapidly to the height required, then stops growing. Life is seldom as simple as that, and it is the quick-growing plants that probably give hedges a bad name. Those that grow very quickly (and few grow quicker than Leyland cypress, × *Cupressocyparis leylandii*) generally go on growing far beyond the ideal height. They can be contained by early and formative pruning (see page 75), but they will still require quite severe trimming each year to keep them within bounds.

If a tall screen is required, however, the widely planted Leyland cypress is worth serious consideration – it can put on 1 m (3 ft) of growth in a year, which is fast by any standards. But the golden form *C.l.* 'Castlewellan' will look less mundane, and it is a little less vigorous.

Alternatives for a tall evergreen hedge or screen that can be clipped neatly really lie among other conifers. *Thuja plicata* 'Atrovirens' is also fast (though not as rapid as the Leyland cypress), but easier to control at a moderate height. It also shoots well from cuts made into old wood, which many conifers will not.

Other good screening conifers of more moderate growth and size to consider, though still relatively quick-growing, are some of the varieties of Lawson's cypress. Two good ones are *Chamaecyparis lawsoniana* 'Allumii' and *C.l.* 'Fletcheri' (blue-grey).

Bear in mind that even the quickest-growing hedges will take about three years to reach the required height and fill out enough to make a really respectable hedge. They are best clipped before they reach the required height (see page 75), to ensure a bushy base, even if this means they take a little longer to reach the required height.

If the hedge is required simply as a screen, perhaps to hide a garage wall, or an unsightly outbuilding, other forms of screens may be more suitable. A self-clinging ivy may do the job, or other climbers grown up a trellis may be more appropriate. Tall bamboos are also worth considering if hedge-like dense growth is required. Some of the taller ones, such as *Arundinaria murieliae*, will grow quickly to form a tall, dense thicket, and you don't need to keep pruning!

PLANTING A HEDGE

Hedges are frequently planted without sufficient thought and preparation – there is only one opportunity to provide the plants with good growing conditions, and they will be there for a long time. Careful planting will also ensure that the plants get off to a good start: they will be able to take care of themselves once established, but are very vulnerable during the first year.

Container-grown plants can be planted at any time

when the ground is not frozen or waterlogged, but frequently hedging plants are sold bare-root. This can reduce the cost of a hedge considerably (hedging plants are often sold in a separate area at garden centres, and though the plants may be a bit smaller, they are often much cheaper than the same species or varieties displayed in the shrub section). As lots of plants are needed for a hedge, it is worth buying these smaller hedging plants, which will usually catch up the larger ones within a few seasons. If buying bare-root plants, however, it is important to plant deciduous ones when they are dormant – mid autumn to early winter, or late winter and early spring are good times. Evergreens, which are usually sold in pots, are best planted in spring.

Prepare the ground thoroughly before planting. Skim off any weeds or grass and fork out any deep-rooted perennial weeds, then take out a trench about 60 cm (2 ft) wide and the depth of the spade's blade. Incorporate as much garden compost, well-rotted manure, or other organic material as you can spare, then fork this into the bottom of the trench. Return the topsoil, adding a bucketful of rotted manure or garden compost and a handful of bonemeal to each 1 m (3 ft) run of trench (or use a slow-release fertilizer at the rate recommended by the manufacturer), working it into the soil.

If the soil is heavy clay, work a couple of bucketfuls of coarse sand or grit into the same area.

Soak the roots of bare-root plants for about three hours before planting; water the compost in container-grown plants and allow it to soak thoroughly before removing the plants from their pots.

Always use a garden line to ensure that you plant a straight hedge! Recommended spacings are given in the entries for particular plants, starting on page 77, but if a particularly dense hedge is required, perhaps to keep out animals, or on a very exposed site where extra wind protection is required, a double row can be planted. Stagger the two rows so that the plants in one row fall half way between plants in the other one, spacing the rows about 38 cm (15 in) apart.

Container-grown plants should be planted in a hole a little larger than the root-ball so that a few roots around the edge can be teased out. Plant at the original depth, or just slightly deeper so that soil can be pulled over the root-ball to reduce the chance of it drying out. Bare-root plants should be planted in holes large enough to take the roots spread out. Cover them with fine soil, firming it as the hole is filled. Use your heel to ensure the soil is firmly settled around the plants.

The success of a newly planted hedge depends largely on ensuring that the soil does not dry out. Unless the ground is wet, the plants should always be watered in thoroughly after planting. Just as important is subsequent watering whenever the soil becomes dry. Be prepared to do this for the first season of growth. If possible, apply a thick mulch of garden compost or well rotted manure along the hedge, which will help to conserve moisture as well as inhibit weeds.

The effect of competition from weeds should never be underestimated, especially during the first couple of seasons. Laying strips of black polythene along the planting row, either side of the plants and as close together as possible in the centre, will conserve moisture and suppress weeds very effectively. It can make a significant difference to how quickly the hedge becomes established.

On a very exposed site, perhaps where the hedge is itself being planted to provide shelter, some initial protection may be required. Chestnut paling or a wattle fence on the prevailing windward side is ideal.

EARLY TRAINING

Most hedges require a light trimming by the end of the first summer. Cut back the leading shoots to an even height, and trim back any long sideshoots that grow beyond the line of the hedge (it is worth fixing a string between two canes to produce the 'edge', and prune back any that go over the line). Even if you have a hedgetrimmer, use secateurs or shears for the early shaping. Let the growth extend by say 15–23 cm (6–9 in) each year until the required height has been reached. If you let the leading shoot grow straight up to the required height and then prune, the growth will be less dense low down, and it may be difficult to achieve a well-shaped hedge of the required height.

Unless a hedge is particularly required as a screen, don't let it become too tall, otherwise cutting will become more of a chore. If possible, keep it reasonably narrow too. A hedge 1.2 m (4 ft) high and 30 cm (1 ft) across the top will represent 25% less cutting than one just 30 cm (1 ft) taller and broader. The modest reduction in height has another benefit, as it is feasible for most people to cut the top of a 1.2 m (4 ft) hedge without having to stand on anything, yet to cut a 1.5 m (5 ft) hedge it may be necessary to use ladders or some other support.

Most hedges are flat-topped, but a gradual taper towards the top, to produce a wedge-shaped or rounded profile, will look particularly smart and it will be less likely to be damaged by snow (the weight of which can break or spoil the shape of a vulnerable hedge). This formative shaping should be taken into account as you trim the hedge during the first few seasons.

HEDGETRIMMING TIPS

COLLECTING THE CLIPPINGS

A tiring, messy, and sometimes dusty job. Make it easier by laying a sheet of polythene along the base of the hedge, or use a canvas or plastic carrying sheet for the same purpose. Most of the clippings can then simply be collected up by folding in the corners.

LARGE-LEAVED HEDGES

These types of hedges, such as laurels, are often left looking scarred and ugly if clipped with shears or a hedgetrimmer. The cut leaves are conspicuous and tend to turn brown at the cut edge. Prune with secateurs for a neater finish.

FOR A STRAIGHT AND LEVEL HEDGE

Use string guidelines and clip to these. If you find this difficult, stretch the string along at the trimming height for the top of the hedge, and trim the whole of the top to this height first. Then remove the string and trim the sides by eye. An uneven side will be far less conspicuous than an uneven top.

SELECTING A HEDGE

The following descriptions will be useful for deciding which type of hedge is most likely to be suitable for your requirements. To make the list practical and helpful, all the plants have been grouped as either formal or informal, and further divided into one of three height groups. There is inevitably some overlap, both in heights and whether formal or informal: much depends on how the hedge is planted and trained.

A formal hedge has a crisp outline and is usually closely trimmed – yew, box and privet are popular examples, though some large-leaved plants can be treated as formal hedges too. Small-leaved species are usually clipped with shears or a hedgetrimmer. An informal hedge is usually looser in outline, and shaping is often done by pruning with secateurs. Most flowering or berrying hedges are informal, as tight clipping would remove the flowers.

Dwarf hedges in this text are taken to mean a low hedge of 60 cm (2 ft) or less, *medium hedges* up to 1.2 m (4 ft) and *tall hedges* 1.5 m (5 ft) or more. These are heights at which the plants tend to make the best hedges, but many medium hedges (such as privet) will also make tall hedges if allowed to do so; tall hedges include some that will make tall screens, and where they are likely to make hedges more than 1.8 m (6 ft) tall, this is mentioned in the text.

DWARF FORMAL HEDGES

Berberis thunbergii 'Atropurpurea Nana'
Small bronze-red leaves, turning vivid red before they fall in autumn, and small bright red berries if not clipped too tightly. For a medium hedge there is a taller form, which is otherwise the same. Clip in late winter. Deciduous. Plant 38 cm (15 in) apart.

Box. *See Buxus*

Buxus sempervirens 'Suffruticosa' (dwarf box)
The small glossy green leaves of the dwarf box can be

trimmed closely to produce a compact edging like those used in earlier times for knot gardens. Be careful to choose this variety, however, as other varieties suitable for hedges grow much taller. Trim in mid or later summer. Evergreen. Plant 23 cm (9 in) apart.

Santolina chamaecyparissus (cotton lavender)

A faster-growing and cheaper alternative to box for a very dwarf formal clipped edging, though it is more difficult to keep compact and tidy. The silvery, feathery foliage is very attractive, however, and it makes a bright and charming dwarf formal edging or miniature hedge. It will produce yellow button-like flowers, but if you let it flower the shape and foliage colour seem to deteriorate, so it's best to trim them off. The species will make a hedge up to 60 cm (2 ft) high, the variety *S.c.* 'Nana' only half this height. The main trimming should be done in mid spring. Evergreen. Plant 25 cm (10 in) apart; 23 cm (9 in) for *S.c.* 'Nana'.

MEDIUM FORMAL HEDGES

Berberis thunbergii 'Atropurpurea'

See *B.t.* 'Atropurpurea Nana' on page 77 for description. Trim in late winter. Deciduous. Plant 45 cm (18 in) apart.

Box. See *Buxus*

Buxus sempervirens (box)

B.s. 'Handsworthensis' is the variety usually recommended for a medium-sized hedge. It has typical box foliage (small evergreen leaves). Trim in mid or late summer. Evergreen. Plant 45 cm (18 in) apart.

Ligustrum (privet)

The privet is one of the most widely planted hedges and needs no introduction. There are several species and varieties, the most common of which is *L. ovalifolium*.

L.o. 'Aureum' is gold with a green central splash (some leaves are completely yellow), and a more attractive plant than the green version. Another golden privet that can be used is *L. vulgare* 'Aureum', which has dull yellow leaves. The golden ones are less vigorous than the green privets, which can mean a little less cutting. Privets greatly impoverish the soil, so do not grow them if you want to plant close to the hedge. Trim monthly from late spring to late summer. Evergreen in mild winters, otherwise semi-evergreen. Plant 38 cm (15 in) apart.

Lonicera nitida (shrubby honeysuckle)

The variety to use for a hedge is *L.n.* 'Fertilis', which has an erect habit. The very small leaves make it ideal for tight formal clipping, but like the privet it requires lots of attention to keep it looking neat and tidy. Trim monthly from late spring to late summer. Evergreen. Plant 38 cm (15 in) apart.

Privet. See *Ligustrum*.

Senecio 'Sunshine'

A pleasant shrub with downy silver leaves, and bright yellow daisy-type flowers. Although not often grown as a hedge, it makes a refreshing change where conditions suit: a mild area and full sun. It generally does well in coastal areas. Prune in early spring. Evergreen. Plant 45 cm (18 in) apart.

Shrubby honeysuckle. See *Lonicera*

TALL FORMAL HEDGES

Some of the species listed here will make tall screens, much higher than a 1.8 m (6 ft) hedge, but for screening or a tall windbreak plant 1.5 m (5 ft) apart instead of the spacing given, and if possible plant two (staggered) rows. If necessary, alternate trees can be removed when the branches touch.

Beech. See *Fagus sylvatica*

Carpinus betulus (hornbeam)
A hornbeam hedge resembles beech, but is a better choice for heavy clay soils. It is a good choice for an exposed site. Trim in winter or late summer. Deciduous, but the leaves hang late. Plant 45 cm (18 in) apart.

Chamaecyparis lawsoniana (Lawson's cypress)
The Lawson cypress is a conifer that comes in many forms, from dwarfs to huge trees, and in a surprising range of colours and shades. It is important to choose suitable varieties: good ones include 'Allumii' (flattened sprays of bluish-grey foliage), 'Fletcheri' (bluish-grey but a slow-grower), 'Pembury Blue' (a striking silvery-blue), and 'Green Hedger' (rich green). Trim in late summer. Evergreen. Plant 60 cm (2 ft) apart.

Crataegus (hawthorn)
Considered by many to be more of a farm hedge than one for the garden, but a well-maintained hawthorn hedge can be very impressive. It is sometimes used in a mixed hedge (usually with beech or hornbeam, privet and holly). It makes a very tough barrier, and the creamy flowers in spring are followed by the haws which last into winter if they have not been clipped off. For a neat garden hedge you will lose most of these when you trim it in mid or late summer. Deciduous. Plant 45 cm (18 in) apart.

× *Cupressocyparis leylandii* (Leyland cypress)
One of the most widely planted of all conifers, mainly because of its fast growth. Will make a tall screen if allowed, and will be difficult to keep below about 2.4 m (8 ft). A large Leyland cypress hedge of this height can look rather dark, but the golden variety 'Castlewellan' is

less oppressive, and a little less vigorous. Trim in late summer. Evergreen. Plant 60 cm (2 ft) apart.

Cupressus macrocarpa (Monterey cypress)
The one to grow for a bright coniferous hedge is *C.m.* 'Goldcrest', which has yellow feathery foliage. It is fast growing and useful for coastal areas. Trim in mid or late summer. Evergreen. Plant 60 cm (2 ft) apart.

Dawn redwood. See *Metasequoia glyptostroboides*

Euonymus japonicus
An unspectacular hedge in many ways, with fairly large plain green leaves, but very useful for coastal areas. The variety 'Ovatus Aureus' is more decorative, with leaves margined and suffused yellow; it tends to be slow growing and is usually grown as a medium hedge. Clip in early summer. Evergreen. Plant 45 cm (18 in) apart.

Fagus sylvatica (beech)
Although not suitable for a very small garden, beech is one of the very best hedges, a good screen (despite being deciduous), excellent as a windbreak, and easily clipped to a formal shape. It tolerates alkaline (chalky) soils well, and will withstand an exposed position. The ordinary green-leaved form is attractive, but one of the purple-leaved varieties such as 'Riversii' is more interesting. You could try interplanting the two. Clip in late summer, but if any major pruning is necessary tackle this in late winter. Deciduous, but the old brown leaves will often hang right through the winter. Plant 45 cm (18 in) apart.

Griselinia littoralis
A charming foliage hedging plant, but only suitable for mild areas, where it does especially well in coastal districts. Apple green foliage that always looks fresh. Prune in mid or late summer. Evergreen. Plant 60 cm (2 ft) apart.

Hawthorn. See *Crataegus*

Hornbeam. See *Carpinus betulus*

Leyland cypress. See × *Cupressocyparis leylandii*

Metasequoia glyptostroboides (dawn redwood)
A fast-growing and potentially very tall conifer that particularly likes moist soils. The foliage is bright green during the summer but turns a tawny pink or old gold in autumn. Unusually for a conifer, it loses its leaves in the winter, which limits its uses as a year-round screen. Trim in mid or late summer. Deciduous. Plant 60 cm (2 ft) apart.

Monterey cypress. See *Cupressus macrocarpa*

Taxus baccata (yew)
A classic plant for formal hedges, and one of the very finest for any garden. It has a reputation for being slow, but this is a merit when you have to clip it, and it is not as slow in the early years as its reputation would have us believe. Does best on a well-drained soil.

The common yew is green, but *T.b.* 'Elegantissima' is a golden form that clips well.

Yew is not a good choice as a boundary where grazing animals might try to eat it, as it can be poisonous.

Yew is usually clipped in late summer. Evergreen. Plant 45–60 cm (1½–2 ft) apart.

Thuja plicata 'Atrovirens' (western red cedar)
A fast-growing conifer with bright green foliage. An excellent choice for a tall coniferous hedge. Trim in late summer. Evergreen. Plant 60 cm (2 ft) apart.

Tsuga heterophylla (western hemlock)
One to think about if you want a coniferous hedge that's a bit unusual – it is not widely planted as a hedge but the pale green foliage makes it an attractive choice. Not

ideal for an alkaline (chalky) soil. Trim in late summer. Evergreen. Plant 60 cm (2 ft) apart.

Western hemlock. See *Tsuga heterophylla*

Western red cedar. See *Thuja plicata*

Yew. See *Taxus baccata*

DWARF INFORMAL HEDGES

Calluna vulgaris (heather)
Heathers need little introduction. This type flowers in late summer, usually in shades of pink or white, but it is worth considering one of the varieties with coloured foliage, such as 'Gold Haze' (yellow) or 'Blazeaway' (reddish in winter). 'Robert Chapman' is another good one to try (gold in spring, changing through orange to red; purple flowers).

Although heathers make interesting low dividers (within the garden or perhaps as an edging for an otherwise open plan garden), there are severe limitations. Callunas must have an acid soil (for a neutral soil, try ericas instead), and they tend to deteriorate after a few years. Trim in early spring, keeping the shape while

---

LOW-MAINTENANCE HEDGES

All hedges will require some trimming or pruning, at least once a year if they are to look respectable. Good all-round hedges that will generally be happy and shapely with a once-a-year cut include beech, hornbeam and berberis. All berberis species mentioned in this book qualify.

---

not cutting into old wood if it can be avoided. Evergreen. Plant 30 cm (12 in) apart.

Erica × *darleyensis* (heather)

This is one of the winter-flowering heathers, and useful for that reason. The limitations are as for callunas, however, except that they will grow satisfactorily on a neutral or slightly alkaline soil if necessary. The species has pink flowers, but there are varieties with magenta flowers ('A. T. Johnson' for example) and white flowers (such as 'Silberschmelze'). Trim after flowering (usually late winter or early spring). If trimming is neglected the plants will become straggly and soon require replacing. Evergreen. Plant 30 cm (12 in) apart.

Heather. See *Calluna vulgaris* and *Erica* × *darleyensis*

Lavandula (lavender)

One of the finest informal flowering dwarf hedges, but is likely to require replacing after a time (new plants can be raised from cuttings).

There are several species and varieties, and height and flower colour will depend on which is chosen. 'Hidcote' is a dependable choice, and will make a 'hedge' or edging about 45 cm (1½ ft) tall. Both the grey-green foliage and deep blue flowers are aromatic. It is an ideal dwarf hedge if you want both flower and foliage effect. Trim after flowering. Evergreen. Plant 30 cm (12 in) apart.

Lavender. See *Lavandula*

MEDIUM INFORMAL HEDGES

Crimson dwarf. See *Prunus* × *cistina*

Daisy bush. See *Olearia* × *haastii*

Flowering currant. See *Ribes sanguineum*

THREE FOR FLOWERING

Many flowering shrubs can be used to make an informal hedge, but three of the best for sheer impact are:

Flowering currant (Ribes) (page 86)
Forsythia (page 89)
Potentilla (page 86)

Fuchsia magellanica

This is an almost hardy fuchsia with long, drooping, typically fuchsia-shaped flowers on arching stems. It can flower from mid summer right through till the frosts if conditions are right. It can make a 1.8 m (6 ft) hedge in frost-free areas, but it gets cut back by frost in most places. In very mild districts it will make a spectacular hedge; elsewhere it may be worth trying as an internal divider within the garden – where it is less important if plants do get cut back or killed. Prune in early or mid spring. Deciduous. Plant 45 cm (18 in) apart.

Hebe

Hebes make excellent low or medium heges, worth growing for flowers or foliage (much depends on the species), but only for mild areas. They are not dependably hardy, and even in favourable areas they may be killed in an exceptionally cold winter. For this reason they are best as internal dividers or low informal markers between gardens. Two good ones to consider are *H. anomala* and *H. brachysiphon*, both with small green leaves and white flowers in early and mid summer, but there are others you could experiment with (especially in a mild area). Trim and shape in late spring. Evergreen. Plant 45 cm (18 in) apart.

Mock orange. See Philadelphus

Olearia × *haastii* (daisy bush)

Oval grey-green leaves and masses of white daisy-type flowers from mid summer. An excellent choice for a coastal garden as it tolerates strong winds and salt-laden air. Prune lightly after flowering. Evergreen. Plant 60 cm (2 ft) apart.

Philadelphus (mock orange)

Most philadelphus are grown as large shrubs, mainly for their fragrant white flowers, but *P. coronarius* 'Aureus' is grown primarily for its golden foliage and can be used to make a bright and distinctive hedge. Do not expect a profusion of flowers when growing it as a hedge. Prune after flowering. Deciduous. Plant 45 cm (18 in) apart.

Potentilla

Some of the shrubby potentillas make pretty, informal hedges, which can be clipped to a neat hedge shape if you do not mind sacrificing some of the flowers, which are mostly yellow. Many varieties of *P. fruticosa* are worth trying as a flowering hedge, but two good hybrids are 'Jackman's Variety' (bluish-green foliage, brilliant yellow flowers) and 'Primrose Beauty' (grey-green downy foliage and primrose yellow flowers). They are often in flower for most of the summer. Prune in early spring. Plant 60 cm (2 ft) apart.

Prunus × *cistina* (crimson dwarf)

An ideal low hedge with coppery-red leaves that open blood red in spring. There is a bonus of small pinkish-white flowers in spring. Trim after flowering. Deciduous. Plant 45 cm (18 in) apart.

Ribes sanguineum (flowering currant)

This flowering hedge will look truly spectacular for a week or so in spring, but rather uninspiring for the rest of the year. The flowers, which hang in small clusters, are usually pink or red (there are several varieties). Prune in mid summer. Deciduous. Plant 60 cm (2 ft) apart.

Rosa (rose)

Rose hedges are something that many gardeners dream of having for their beautiful and often fragrant flowers, but there are drawbacks. Rose hedges can be spreading, pruning is a sometimes unpleasant job because of the prickly stems, and in winter they are far from attractive. They do not make practical boundary hedges for the roadside because of their spreading habit and thorny stems, but they can look attractive as an internal hedge, or to divide two properties. Lots of shrub roses, and some tall floribundas, can be used, but very high on any list must be *R. rugosa* – it has bold foliage, big fragrant flowers (deep pink, in early summer and continuing intermittently until autumn) followed by big red hips. Prune in early spring. Deciduous. Plant 60 cm (2 ft) apart.

Rosmarinus (rosemary)

One of the very best informal hedges, but best as an internal divider or as a boundary marker between two gardens, and not suitable for very cold areas. 'Miss Jessopp's Upright' is a good choice for a hedge. Grey-green aromatic foliage and small pale blue flowers in leafy spikes. The flowers start in early spring (even in winter in a very mild year) and continue sporadically until autumn. Trim when flowering is over. Evergreen. Plant 60 cm (2 ft) apart.

Tamarix pentandra (tamarisk)

A pretty, but rather 'feathery' hedge that can be used inland but is primarily a choice for coastal gardens. Sprays of small pink flowers in late summer. Fast-growing. Prune in early spring. Deciduous. Plant 60 cm (2 ft) apart.

TALL INFORMAL HEDGES

Berberis darwinii

A good foliage plant with small holly-shaped glossy green leaves, and the bonus of vivid orange-yellow flowers in mid or late spring. Bluish-purple berries may follow if not trimmed off. The plants are best clipped after flowering. Evergreen. Plant 60 cm (2 ft) apart.

Berberis × stenophylla

An impenetrable and impressive informal hedge in flower, with its arching sprays of yellow flowers in late spring or early summer. Prune after flowering. Evergreen. Plant 60 cm (2 ft) apart.

Cotoneaster

A few cotoneaster species make pleasant if uninspired hedges, useful primarily for their berries. *C. franchetii* (semi-evergreen) has grey-green foliage and orange-red berries on arching stems. *C. lacteus* (evergreen) has long-lasting red berries, and will make a taller hedge than the other two mentioned (well over 1.8 m/6 ft if

---

THREE OF THE BEST EVERGREENS

For a really good formal evergreen hedge, the traditional 'classic' hedging plants yew and box have to be at the top of any shortlist: yew needs a bit of patience, but box is quicker. Holly is more suitable for large gardens than small ones, but makes a really impressive hedge – formal or informal – and depending on the varieties chosen can be green or variegated, and even studded with berries. A slow grower, but worth the wait.

you let it); *C. simonsii* (semi-evergreen) has bright berries that show up well after some of the leaves, which turn scarlet, have fallen. All have white flowers in early summer. Prune off long shoots in summer, trim in winter. Plant 45–60 cm (1½–2 ft) apart.

Elaeagnus
Some elaeagnus species make choice hedges, but they can be slow in the early years. They are useful by the sea, but desirable anywhere. *E.* × *ebbingei* has large dark green, glossy leaves, silvery beneath. For a really dazzling hedge the gold-splashed *E. pungens* 'Maculata' will not disappoint. Prune in late summer. Plant 60 cm (2 ft) apart.

Escallonia macrantha
Another good choice for coastal areas, though it will make a fine hedge inland too. In cold areas it will lose its leaves in winter, and in very unfavourable districts may be killed. Small, glossy green leaves and small rose-crimson flowers in early summer. There are many hybrids, and two good ones for hedging are 'Crimson Spire' and 'Red Hedger'. Prune after flowering. Semi-evergreen. Plant 45 cm (18 in) apart.

Firethorn. See Pyracantha

Forsythia
One of the most popular flowering hedges, and absolutely eyecatching for a couple of weeks in spring. Unfortunately it is uninspiring for the rest of the year. Better as a dividing hedge between two gardens than as a roadside hedge – unless you plant it behind a low wall. The bright yellow bells are a well-known part of the spring garden scene. A good variety is 'Lynwood'. Prune after flowering (if necessary tip back any very long shoots in late summer). Deciduous. Plant 60 cm (2 ft) apart.

SOMETHING GREY?

For an ever-grey rather than an evergreen, try *Senecio* 'Sunshine' (page 79), or for a dwarf hedge *Santolina chamaecyparissus* (page 78). Rosemary (page 87) is not actually grey, but has a distinctive grey-green appearance.

Holly. See *Ilex*

Hippophae rhamnoides (sea buckthorn)
A rather stark hedge in many ways, but one to consider for an exposed coastal area as it is wind resistant and tolerates salt spray. Linear silvery-white leaves and clusters of orange berries that can last well into winter. The flowers are insignificant. You need plants of both sexes for berries, but in a hedge where there are a lot of plants this should not be a problem.

Ilex (holly)
Although holly has been placed here under informal hedges, it can be tightly clipped to make a first-rate formal hedge (but it takes very many years to make a large, formally clipped hedge). It is slow even as an informal hedge. Holly is great as a barrier – not only because it will make dense growth, but because of its prickles, though some varieties, such as *I. aquifolium* 'J. C. van Tol' have almost spineless leaves (useful for the safety of passers-by). Variegated varieties also make attractive hedges. It is usual to plant a mixed hedge of male and female varieties for berry production (berries are not usually a feature of tightly-clipped formal holly hedges). Prune in late summer. Evergreen. Plant 60 cm (2 ft) apart.

Prunus laurocerasus (common laurel, cherry laurel)
A vigorous plant useful for screening, especially in gloomy areas where many hedges will not thrive. Large evergreen leaves and white flower spikes in mid or late spring. Can look oppressive and is too big for most gardens, but useful for difficult places. Prune mid or late summer. Evergreen. Plant 45 cm (18 in) apart.

Prunus lusitanica (Portugal laurel)
Oval dark green leaves, and slender spikes of white flowers in early summer. Uses similar to the common laurel, but a better choice for shallow chalk soils. Prune mid or late summer. Evergreen. Plant 45 cm (18 in) apart.

Pyracantha (firethorn)
This common wall shrub, generally grown for its colourful berries, can also be made into a hedge. Although most species and varieties can be used, *P. rogersiana* is a good one to try. The white flowers in summer are followed by red berries in autumn. *P.* 'Watereri' is another good free-fruiting choice. Prune in spring, and trim again to improve the shape in the summer if necessary. Deciduous. Plant 50 cm (20 in) apart.

Sea buckthorn. See *Hippophae rhamnoides*

Snowberry. See *Symphoricarpos*

***Symphoricarpos* × *doorenbosii* 'White Hedge'**
Not an outstanding hedge, but useful if berries are required for autumn interest. The small white berries are freely produced. Will also make a medium-sized hedge. Prune in late winter or early spring. Deciduous. Plant 45 cm (1½ ft) apart.

MIXING AND MATCHING

Be creative where it seems appropriate. A wall may serve a practical purpose but lack visual appeal, or you may fancy a hedge but want a more instant kind of boundary while it is growing, so why not combine a hedge with a wall? If you think a long stretch of hedge could look boring, why not plant a mixed hedge to add interest? If you want a living boundary but a straight-trimmed hedge lacks appeal, why not plant a row of spaced-out conifers that will retain their shape yet form a practical screen and barrier, perhaps with a decorative low wall at the base? These are just some of the ways in which you can express your own individuality and sense of design when it comes to boundaries.

WALLS WITH HEDGES

Walls can combine effectively with hedges, but only if they are low and the materials blend with the hedge.

Any wall over about 1 m (3 ft) will spoil the shape and appearance of the hedge, and often a low one about 30 cm (1 ft) high is particularly effective – it fills the gappy area that many hedges suffer from at the base, will not spoil the shape of the hedge, and will be relatively inexpensive and quick to construct. A low wall like this is often best made from reconstituted stone walling blocks in a light colour, to help to give a crisp, light outline – dark bricks can look insignificant once the hedge grows tall.

A wall about 60–90 cm (2–3 ft) high is best combined with a formal hedge that is neatly trimmed, and a golden privet can look particularly striking with brick.

Tall walls like this are often useful for informal flowering hedges such as forsythia and flowering currant, however, as the wall provides an effective barrier and a crisp outline that neither of these shrubs can match. These plants make magnificent hedges for a couple of weeks each spring, but can look uninspiring for the rest of the summer, and decidedly redundant during the winter when the stems are bare. A low wall in front of them comes into its own when a flowering hedge like this is going through its 'off' phase.

A red chaenomeles (flowering quince) hedge also looks good behind a low wall, and can make this a very worthwhile hedge even though it cannot be recommended on its own because of the gappy nature of the base and lack of year-round cover.

For something more adventurous, try a three-way mix: alternate plants of flowering currant and forsythia and build a low wall in front. These two shrubs flower at about the same time, and can look really stunning together.

Bear in mind that combined walls and hedges take up space, and in a small garden where space is at a premium, it may be better to settle for a low wall that will not cast too much shade, so that you can plant flowers in the bed in front of it.

SPACED SHRUBS AND CONIFERS

Rows of columnar, pencil-like conifers, such as *Juniperus scopulorum* 'Skyrocket' and *Juniperus communis* 'Hibernica' can be planted to form a screen of individual plants. These two will need no clipping in the early years, as they have natural narrow and upright growth, but with age you may have to clip each individual plant lightly to retain their distinct shapes. Spacing needs thought with this type of living screen, as you do not want to plant them so close that they merge into each other like a hedge, but you need them close enough to touch within a few years.

A similar kind of screen can be produced with more conically shaped conifers, perhaps alternating green and gold varieties of the same species (do not mix different species as their growth rates may be too uneven). Because conically shaped plants will become broad at the base they require wider initial spacing, which may produce a sparse appearance for a few years. Constructing a very low wall in front can help to give this kind of boundary a stronger sense of purpose in the early years.

MIXED HEDGES

If you have a very large garden, and a lot of patience, a mixed hedge that incorporates many different kinds of plants, such as beech, hawthorn, quickthorn and privet can look very pleasing, but in a small garden it is best to restrain your enthusiasm and keep to just two different plants, such as purple and green beech, or green and variegated holly.

INDEX

The page numbers in *italic* refer to line illustrations